353

1650
ⓑ

"The Boy Will Come to Nothing!"

"The Boy Will Come to Nothing!"

Freud's Ego Ideal and Freud as Ego Ideal

Leonard Shengold, M.D.

Yale University Press   New Haven and London

The following previously published articles, in revised and greatly expanded form, have been used as chapters of this book. I wish to thank the original publishers for graciously granting their permission to use this material here.

1. "Freud and Joseph." In M. Kanzer, ed., *The Unconscious Today,* 473–94. New York: International Univ. Press, 1971.

2. "A Parapraxis of Freud's in Relation to Karl Abraham." *Amer. Imago* 29 (1972): 123–59.

3. "The Freud/Jung Letters." *J. Amer. Psychoanal. Assn.* 24 (1976): 669–83.

Designed by Sonia L. Scanlon
Set in Baskerville type by DEKR Corporation.
Printed in the United States of America by Vail-Ballou Press, Binghamton, New York.

Library of Congress Cataloging-in-Publication Data
Shengold, Leonard.
    The boy will come to nothing : Freud's ego ideal and Freud as ego ideal / Leonard Shengold.
        p. cm.
    Includes bibliographical references and index.
    ISBN 0-300-05684-2
    1. Freud, Sigmund, 1856–1939—Psychology. 2. Freud, Sigmund, 1856–1939—Influence. 3. Ego-ideal. I. Title.
    [DNLM: 1. Freud, Sigmund, 1856–1939. 2. Famous Persons. 3. Identification (Psychology) 4. Psychoanalytic Interpretation. 5. Superego. WM 460.5.I4 S546b]
    BF109.F74S44   1993
    150.19'52—dc20
    DNLM/DLC
    for Library of Congress   92-49700
                                         CIP

A catalogue record for this book is available from the British Library. The paper in this book meets the guidelines for permanence and durability of the Committee on Production Guidelines for Book Longevity of the Council on Library Resources.

10 9 8 7 6 5 4 3 2 1

To Jeffrey Stephen Shengold

Analysts of society or art regularly neglect what is, for the parts of it their explanation is able to take account of, and then go on the assumption that their explanation is all that there is. (If the methods of some disciplines deal only with, say, what is quantitatively measurable, and something is not quantitatively measurable, then the thing does not exist for that discipline—after a while the lower right-hand corner of the inscription gets broken off, and it reads *does not exist*.) But if someone has a good enough eye for an explanation he finally sees nothing inexplicable, and can begin every sentence with that phrase dearest to all who professionally understand: It is no accident that. . . . We should love explanations well, but the truth better; and often the truth is that there *is* no explanation, that so far as we know it is an accident that. . . . The motto of the city of Hamburg is: *Navigare necesse est, vivere non necesse.* A critic might say to himself: for me to know *what* the work of art is, is necessary; for me to explain *why* it is what it is, is not always necessary nor always possible.

—Randall Jarrell,
  "Malraux and the Statues at Bamberg"

CONTENTS

PREFACE

I hope I won't confuse the reader by beginning this book about Sigmund Freud with a quotation that concerns two great Russian writers who had little to do with him. Maxim Gorki is describing the thoughts attendant on his hearing that

LEO TOLSTOY IS DEAD.

A telegram came containing the commonest of words: "is dead." It struck me to the heart: I cried with pain and anger, and now half crazy, I imagine him as I know and saw him. . . . I once saw him as, perhaps, no one has ever seen him. I was walking over to him at Gaspra along the coast, and . . . on the shore among the stones I saw his smallish angular figure in a gray, crumpled, ragged suit and crumpled hat. He was sitting with his head on his hands, the wind blowing the silvery hairs of his beard through his fingers: he was looking into the distance out to sea, and the little greenish waves rolled up obediently to his feet and fondled them as if they were telling something about themselves to the old magician. It was a day of sun and cloud, and the shadows of the clouds glided over the stones, and with the stones the old man grew now bright and now dark. The boulders were large, riven by cracks and covered with smelly seaweed; there had been a high tide. He, too, seemed to me like an old stone come to life, who knows all the beginnings and ends of things, who considers when and what will be the end of the stone, of the grasses of the earth, of the waters of the sea, and of the whole universe from the pebble to the sun. . . . Suddenly, in a moment of madness, I felt, "It is possible, he will get up, wave his hand, and the sea will become solid and glassy, the stones will begin to move and cry out, everything around him will come to life, acquire a voice and speak in their different voices of themselves, of him, against him." I cannot express in words what I felt rather than thought at that moment; in my soul there was joy and fear, and then everything blended in one happy thought: "I am not an orphan on the earth, so long as this man lives on it." (Gorki 1910, 37–38)

Maxim Gorki was very much an orphan. He had a terrible childhood. After his father died, when the boy was four, he and his mother lived in a provincial town in the house of his brutal maternal grandfather, a "house that seethed with mutual hostility" (Gorki 1915, 22). His two uncles hated and feared their domineering father ("my mother [and I] arrived on the very day when her brothers demanded the distribution of the property from their father. . . . They were afraid that my mother would claim the dowry intended for her, but withheld by my grandfather because she had married secretly and against his wish" [23]). His mother was depressed and withdrawn. She did her best to protect the boy from his grandfather, who flogged him until he lost consciousness. Unable to help, she left, apparently with some man, abandoning Maxim. She returned unpredictably for short periods from time to time. Once she came back pregnant and quarreled dramatically with her father. Maxim's grandfather had earlier told the boy that his mother had run away and didn't care about him.[1] The uncles were brutes to their wives and children. Gorki's father had been kind, and so was his maternal grandmother ("a dark, tender, wonderfully interesting person . . . from the very first day I made friends with her" [Gorki 1915, 4–5]), in whose bed he slept and toward whom he expresses gratitude as the only one in the terrible household who enabled him to know that happiness was possible. His grandfather continued to beat him, but he also taught him to read.

Gorki started to work for his living before he was a teenager. His mother died of tuberculosis when he was eleven, and

a few days after his mother's funeral, his grandfather said to

1. Maxim Gorki's real name was Alexey Peshkov. Like many authors—and orphans—he rechristened himself, calling himself by his dead and idealized father's first name, Maxim, and his father's nickname, *Gorky* (= bitter). He records his grandfather's unforgettable words thus: "[Grandfather:] 'That mother of yours does not care what becomes of you, my lad.' Grandmother started. 'Oh father, why do you say such things?' 'I ought not to have said it—my feelings got the better of me. Oh, what a girl that is for going astray!'" (Gorki 1915, 128).

him, "Alexey, you're not a medal: you can't go hanging from my neck. Go out into the world and earn your own living." Alexey was eleven. He obeyed. (Troyat 1986, 8)

He worked at a series of odd jobs, wandering from place to place, living like a nomad. He became a revolutionary. At nineteen he attempted suicide. As a youth, he walked the more than two hundred miles to Moscow from Nizhni-Novgorod (now called Gorki) and went directly to try to see Tolstoy to ask questions about his political and religious beliefs. Vladimir Nabokov says,

Tolstoy was not at home, but the Countess invited him into the kitchen and treated him to coffee and rolls. She observed that a great number of bums kept coming to see her husband, to which Gorki politely agreed. (1940, 298)

Tolstoy is the chief subject of a small masterpiece by Gorki, "Reminiscences of Tolstoy, Chekhov, and Andreyev," which shows how much the older man meant to him. It was a complicated relationship between a talented, self-taught writer just beginning to be successful when the two actually started their friendship and a Great Man, the greatest writer of the age, founder of a religious, philosophical, and social movement, as famous as the czar. Gorki was fascinated by Tolstoy, whom he alternately idealized, loved, and hated. He could be acutely critical of the older man. But, as one can tell from the excerpt I have quoted, even after Tolstoy's death, Gorki kept him alive in his mind, in his soul, as part of himself. In the quoted passage, Tolstoy is the whole world for Gorki, God and grandfather and grandmother and father and mother—perhaps above all mother. Yet this intensity was of course transient, and Gorki easily sustained the actual loss (while holding Tolstoy in his mind)[2] and went on to do some of his best work in his autobio-

2. In a letter written after Tolstoy's death, Gorki says, "[Tolstoy's] flight from his house and his family made me feel skeptical and almost angry with him . . . because I know his old need to suffer [in order] to put himself in agreement with his religious ideas and his preaching. . . . You know how much I hate that kind of sermon recommending a passive attitude toward life, and you must realize how harmful those Buddhist ideas are in a nation deeply impregnated with fatalism. . . . And suddenly a telegram . . . announcing Leo Nikolayevich's [Tolstoy's] death. For five minutes I felt very strange. Then I sobbed. I locked myself in my room and wept desperately all day. I have never felt so much an orphan as I did that day; I have never felt such sadness over a man's death. . . . The most beautiful, most powerful and greatest man has left our lives. . . . It is not only his wife who has been

graphical writing. Gorki was subsequently to be done in by a revenant of his terrible grandfather: the murderous, stone-hearted
Stalin.

This book is about Sigmund Freud, another Great Man who is
dead and who is kept alive not only through his work but in his
person, as part of the soul of many others trying to ward off
orphanage, of generations of intellectuals, and especially of students of the mind. For psychoanalysts, he is "our" Freud, and this
has led me to ask what one person, especially a great person, means
to another. This seems a query that can be answered simply, but it
leads to nothing less than the complexities of the development of
the mind. The psychoanalyst usually responds[3] to any question by
beginning genetically, seeking for origins: connecting with the
child's early universe, which starts in chaos and develops to some
vaguely global awareness of merger with another, then to a sense
of a grandiose self whose omnipotence is connected intimately with
(and, contradictorily, dependent on) an idealized, all-powerful
Other (godlike, as Tolstoy on the shore appeared to Gorki). A
primal parent is first separated out from the initial merged self/par-
ent; usually this is the mother. The father becomes important later.
The two at first retain their godlike powers, but these (along with
the grandiosity of the self) shrink as time and maturation proceed.
Much of the child's subsequent psychic development depends on
identifications (Freud calls them secondary identifications) with
others, starting with the parents (now perceived more realistically)—taking them in to become part of one's mind and self. In
the small but expanding psychic universe of the nursery, siblings
also take an inordinate, clamorous, and largely unwelcome part.

Our natures, our instinctual drives, make for conflicts that lead
inevitably to dangers based on our initial helplessness and dependency. The conflicts arise from the intensity of our needs and the
resultant rage at unavoidable frustrations. Because of this rage
(which Freud feels is part of our instinctual heritage as well as the
result of frustration), we seek to rid ourselves of the very Others
we cannot do without. These others as part of the self are constantly

widowed, it is also Russian literature. . . . It is a judge who has left. I even miss the
prophet intensely, yet I disliked him!" (quoted in Troyat 1986, 116).

3. But of course this is only one psychoanalyst's answer. For reasons of brevity,
I am presenting a sketch of a child's early psychic development in a tone of certainty
although the nature of this development probably can never be accurately grasped
and is therefore of necessity fraught with mystery, controversy, and speculation.

transformed and modified as we mature, but even the earliest registrations are never lost and can reappear transiently and take over their former power. Thus, under the threat of his loss, Tolstoy reappears for Gorki as the godlike, idealized primal parent, eternal as stone. For the self to become strong and independent, the initial godlike Others must be assimilated within so that they can largely be replaced in contemporary life by others—real people, eventually people outside the primal family, who can also be meaningful and can give and receive love.

These substitute others are needed (with less urgency than their parental antecedents) and can and should become precious. Dependency continues, but optimally it recedes with the consolidation of an independent sense of identity. We are still constantly surrounded by the realistic prospect of losses and must regress not only in reaction to them but also in anxious anticipation of them, for our instinctual nature ties us to murder as well as to desire and fear. We make use of a series of others, beginning with our actual parents, as gods; or as doubles; then others as substitute parents; substitute siblings; as children and substitute children—all transient replacements for the original primal narcissistic Others toward whom we return in death. For the fulfillment of our needs and for the continuing nourishment of our souls, we also use Great Men and Great Women from the past and the present, even from fiction—as well as friends, lovers, acquaintances on whom we become dependent—taking them in as parts of our mind (and thus conferring on them, consciously or unconsciously, a transitory narcissistic kind of greatness). We make our own changeable psychic versions of them, to guard us against feeling like orphans in a hostile or indifferent universe of stone.

ACKNOWLEDGMENTS

I feel especially indebted to a number of helpful readers of various large parts of the manuscript drafts of this book for their useful suggestions, admonitions, and encouragement. These ego ideal figures are Shelley Orgel, Warren Poland, Vann Spruiell, Edward Weinshel, and, above all, my wife. Gladys Topkis, my editor at Yale University Press, had her usual magical effect not only on the quality of the prose but on the book's very structure. She, my manuscript editor, Lawrence Kenney, and my wife read every word of the book; their corrections were accepted, and their suggestions for improvements were seriously considered and generally followed. I am grateful to the helpful and friendly staff at Yale University Press. My ego ideal has been enriched by contacts with many colleagues—so many that I am afraid I can give only an incomplete list: Sandy Abend, Sam Abrams, Mike Allison, Jack Arlow, Hal Blum, Dale Boesky, Charlie Brenner, Vic Calef, Larry Chalfin, Bill Console, Homer Curtis, Alan Eisnitz, Robert Fliess, Anna Freud, Stan Goodman, Paul Gray, Jerry Jacobson, Betty Joseph, Mark Kanzer, Jerry Levine, Roy Lilleskov, Shelley Orgel, Leo Rangell, Owen Renik, Max Schur, Hannah Segal, Austin Silber, Vann Spruiell, Arthur Valenstein, Bob Wallerstein, Ed Weinshel. Infusions have been steadily received from my participation in CAPS (Center for Advanced Psychoanalytic Study) at Princeton—from its leader, Sam Guttman, and the members of my CAPS group: Steve Ablon, Hugh Dickinson, Joan Erle, Manny Furer, Stan Goodman, Paul Gray, Alex Harrison, Milton Horowitz, Dan Jaffe, Charlie Kligerman, Arnie Pfeffer, Sam Ritvo, Herb Schlesinger, Austin Silber, Al Solnit. I do not have the space to list those whom I have met and been influenced by in connection with my attendance at the Anna Freud Centre, and my positions with the American and the International Psychoanalytical Associations. There are many whom I have left out—my bibliography includes and even features some of them as well as many I have never met but whose writings have meant much to me. And I have learned so much from my students and, most of all, from my patients.

"The Boy Will Come to Nothing!"

1

MAKING GREAT MEN OURS

To us he is no more a person
Now but a whole climate of opinion.

W. H. Auden, "In Memory of
Sigmund Freud"

I first heard Auden's poem on the death of Freud when it was read aloud to me as a sixteen-year-old Columbia College freshman by my humanities teacher, Lionel Trilling. Auden's "us" meant intellectuals with open enough minds to be involved in critical observation and especially self-observation, and open enough hearts to be able to be so passionately. Trilling idealized Freud (but not uncritically), and I idealized Trilling (completely uncritically). I had already read Freud's "Introductory Lectures" and had felt convinced that I wanted to follow him and become a psychoanalyst. But to me, an ignorant boy from the provinces, being with Lionel Trilling was like being with a living Freud: Mind incarnate. Outside of books, I had encountered no one like him.

I was able, after some time, to see flaws. One of my friends, a private school graduate more practiced in the classics than I, had done a good deal of reading of literary critics. Having become adept at the ad hominem attacks he had come upon in his perusal of the skirmishes of literary politics, he was delighted to point out to me the great man's narcissism as well as what he declared to be our teacher's occasional faux pas. "Trilling always looks out of the window and not at us because he likes to show his profile," said my friend. The observation was true, whatever the reason for it. And my friend was quick to indicate the presumption of Trilling's beginning one class with a look of pain and a remark beside the point of the day's topic: "Mozart was dead at my age." *I* thought that Trilling's occasional theatricality enhanced his teaching. Besides, I felt no great inappropriateness: Trilling was as close to a Mozart as anyone I had ever come across. To me he was a living miracle, a fountainhead of passionate intellectuality, a conduit to great literature. I was also much influenced by Trilling's friend and occasional co-teacher, the brilliant Jacques Barzun. To them I owe my happy introduction to some of the great minds of the West and great characters in literature, many of whom took their places in my picture of the world and became part of the me who fashioned that picture.

Unlike some of Trilling's groupies, I never tried to get to know him personally. This was part of a characteristic shyness that army service and psychoanalysis would reduce if not eliminate. But I also had some perhaps mistaken sense that, as with Freud (and I learned a great deal about Freud from Trilling), I needed some distance to protect the idealization requisite for the retention of a spiritual parent. My inner pictures of and claims upon both great men helped me grow up and loosen my psychic ties with my parents. In psychoanalytic jargon, censored and idealized personal versions of Freud and Trilling became ego ideals and modified my earlier, more fundamental identifications.

"Auden is often a didactic poet," Trilling told us. "You can take notes from his poems."[1] When he said this, I felt he was talking directly to me—although it was actually one of those moments when he was looking out of the window and, according to my friend, showing his profile. Although Trilling disapproved of note taking in his classes, I had at first disregarded this and continued to do so occasionally. I never really used those notes—my surreptitious scribbling was usually illegible. In retrospect I believe that I wanted substantial evidence of what I regarded as an experience of epiphany. I didn't know it then, but later I saw clearly that I had been in a state of idealized love—a crush that had no conscious sexual content.

Being drafted in World War II interrupted my time at college.

1. For example, Auden (1939) says of Freud,

[He] showed us what evil is: not as we thought
Deeds that must be punished, but our lack of faith,
Our dishonest mood of denial,
The concupiscence of the oppressor. (166)

This definition of evil describes the modifying of conscience (superego) that comes when maturation brings wisdom (a development that should be fostered by psychoanalysis); the poetic paragraph could be expanded into a paper on the subject.

When I returned to Columbia I had grown up a good deal; my motivations had changed, the libidinal charge was elsewhere (I met my future wife in one of Barzun's classes), but I still sought out Trilling as a teacher and retained him as an ego ideal.

My first thought was to give this book the title *Our Freud*. By that I mean the Freud, or Freuds, of his literary, scientific, and especially of his psychoanalytic children, his followers. We, those modified by the "whole climate of opinion," each have our own Freud. There are not only personal versions but also differing personal versions of collective Freuds. These exist in dynamic and complex forms, as do all our mental impressions of others and of others in relation to ourselves. These mental representations of other people change along with changes in the representations of our self—that is, in accordance with the shifts in our transferences and projections and identifications.

The personal Freuds are the subject of constant mental (intrapsychic) revision; the collective Freuds are the subject of endless (interpsychic) debate. All followers, as well as biographers and historians, are involved in the vain search for the "real" Freud. If dedicated to finding the truth, no matter what (a conscious goal of any true Freudian), they would feel constantly obliged to sort out the influences of their own needs for Freud. That requires examining the distorting transferences and projections that inevitably modify what is externalized onto Freud to produce an image regarded as my or our Freud.[2] Freud as role model gets internalized, digested, and recast as an alter ego or an ego ideal. This purified image of him, a partial idealization centering on Freud at his best (that is, relatively stripped of primitive, distorting idealization and devaluation and not to be exactly equated with the complex, contradictory, dynamically changeable, occasionally fallible, historical human being "as he actually was"), would be the man about whom W. H. Auden wrote after Freud's death in 1939,

All that he did was to remember
Like the old and be honest like children. (1939, 165)

In this book I want to focus on the universal need for parents that gets partially transformed as we lose the sense of parental omnipresence—an inevitable loss which can make us feel orphaned

2. Transferences: putting onto Freud aspects of one's past relationships with parents or siblings. Projections: putting onto Freud aspects of one's own self.

even when still fully parented. The need soon begins to shift to include figures from the past, from literature, and, most important for healthy development, others beside the parents from the present. This partial displacement functions to shore up our sense of identity, to provide continuity with our past, to become part of our psychic picture of our selves. These substitute figures usually consist of great people from history, mythology, fiction, and contemporary life as well as more ordinary others whom we ephemerally endow with a kind of narcissistic greatness because their emotional propinquity fulfills our need for central importance. This need to absorb the worked-over image of other selves is a continuation of our initial absolute dependence on our parents, not only for bodily care but as part of the requisite physical/psychic interactional and identificatory matrix from which our separate identities are acquired and modified.

To illustrate this need, I will refer to a patient from whom I learned to become aware of it with the dazzling starkness that sometimes emerges from the study of a psychotic. A schizophrenic boy, K., who had been passed from therapist to therapist over a course of many years, was referred to me as one of my first psychotherapy patients. By that time the "boy" was almost thirty but looked seventeen. His wild stare, exotically ill-matched clothes, and bizarre behavior made him a conspicuously psychotic disturber to other patients in the waiting room. Most of them felt sympathetic toward him because of his gentle and childlike look of suffering. But since I shared the waiting room with another psychiatrist whose patients were also being affected, I felt some inner pressure to get rid of K. for my colleague's sake. Perhaps this kind of uneasiness, I initially conjectured, had motivated previous therapists to pass him on quickly to new beginners.

I resisted the pressure and saw K. for about four years. By the time we had to stop I had modified my speculation about why supportive therapy had never lasted very long. His paranoid parents became so upset and angry in response to his achievement of more independence from them that they forced him out of treatment with me despite my protests and warning. K. had reacted to his painful loss of so many parental substitutes (beginning, I learned, with nursemaids who had been dismissed when he became attached to them) by completely erasing them from his memory. He did keep in his memory one of the first psychiatrists he had seen—Dr. G. He remembered few details about the treatment and literally none about Dr. G.'s person. But he could summon up a vague picture of Dr. G. and repeated various things that Dr. G. had said, usually in strangely mechanical but yet incantatory manner, a monotone of awe—as a devout rabbinical student might recite from the Torah.

K.'s therapy with me had in a way started with a recorded transcript from Dr. G. On entering my consultation room for the first time, K. had proffered a very limp hand for a handshake. When he sat down, he recited in a drill sergeant's loud, monotonous voice (issued from an expressionless face), "You don't kiss men! You shake hands with men!" Then K. smiled vaguely and began to tell me (or at least to talk in my general direction) about Dr. G. Dr. G., he said, was "a second Sigmund Freud, the greatest psychiatrist who has ever lived," and Dr. G. had saved his life. K. said, loudly and rather belligerently, that he didn't know how Dr. G. had saved his life, but he had (I could imagine from this fragment the arguments K. might have had with his parents on the subject of the wonderful Dr. G.).

K. was tormented and frightened by his sexual excitement about men. Many of the details of this never became clear, as K. was wont to become very anxious and overexcited when he talked about it. Yet, as an obsessive preoccupation, what could too simply but yet unquestionably be called homosexual arousal kept bursting into his awareness. For many years he had been particularly drawn to the men who worked in a gas station near his home. Thinking about their uniforms, their bending under the opened car hood to examine the motor, their jabbing phallic hoses into gas tank openings (I am supplying my own words for his fragmented expression of these things) could send K. into an excited frenzy during which he would start jumping up and down, shouting, "Gasoline! Gasoline! Gasoline! I smell gasoline!"

K. would occasionally begin the shouting in my consulting room, but most frequently this behavior occurred when he used the bathroom adjoining the patients' waiting room for prolonged bouts of defecation before or after his hour. This activity and venue suggested some of the anal excitement aroused in association with his sexual fantasies. (I felt it also denoted both the shift of the object of his excitement from the gas station attendants onto me and his trying to resist, discharge, and sequester that excitement.) Although I couldn't hear K. in the bathroom myself, his shouting and stamping there were reported to me by other patients. And from what he told me, I knew that K. regarded what he called his "shitting time here" as part of the ritual that denoted his right as a patient. I thought of this right (and rite) as a primitive expression of his belonging to me, or, rather, of my belonging to him—some almost phylogenetically regressive equivalent, as it were, of an animal marking off territory with its excretions. The bathroom ritual, which went on only at his home or in my office, sometimes calmed and sometimes terrified K. When the anxiety got out of control, the shouts of "Gasoline!" would be succeeded by shouts of "Dr. G.!" or "Dr. Shengold!" At these times, I felt, he was crying for help and for merger.

In childhood and early adolescence, K.'s sexual excitement about men had been expressed in action chiefly by his attempts to kiss men he would meet: the attendants at the gas station, his teachers at school, the mailman, salesmen who rang the doorbell at home. This behavior had attracted much unwelcome attention, and the reactive hostility, ridicule, and gossip had finally motivated K.'s parents to take the boy to a psychiatrist or, rather, to one psychiatrist after another until they were lucky enough, or at least K. was lucky enough, to find someone able to deal with them in Dr. G.

The parents' own crazy, persistently unempathic, and hostile attitudes toward K. were well known to me through their repeated provocative, complaining phone calls. Usually they grumbled about K.'s rebellious behavior or about others' reactions to him. Unless it was brought up as the object of others' complaints, they did not seem to notice K.'s array of *bizarreries*—which, I speculated, generally fit in with and reflected the parents' own strangeness. (An example of their communication: although K. was terrified of women and had never shown the slightest sexual or any other kind of interest in them, his parents railed at me because K. did not yet seem ready to settle down, get married, and produce grandchildren.)

The injunction against kissing men that had led to the therapy with me was a remnant of what Dr. G. had told K. The portentous, monotonous delivery was unconsciously intended, I believe, to evoke Dr. G. as a kind of hypnotist who had taken control of his subject. K.'s ritualized recitation was audible evidence of his using internalized (psychically transcribed) bits of his experience with Dr. G. as a kind of poorly assimilated, awkward prosthesis (perhaps accomplished in part by some kind of autohypnotic shift of consciousness) to strengthen his ego and his conscience in order to defend against and obtain control over the dangers attendant on overstimulation. Dr. G. was, transiently and clumsily, part of K., and K. felt he was sharing the benevolent, protective, controlling power of his therapist. K. was unable to describe Dr. G. in any physical way. As I subsequently learned from Dr. G., K. had several times passed him in the neighborhood they shared with no sign of recognition. This had happened both during and after the time Dr. G. treated K. (This cognitive inhibition was repeated in relation to me several years after K. had stopped coming to see me. K. entered an elevator I was in, and when I said hello to him he stared at me as at a stranger.)

But the therapy began with a positive, indeed an idealizing attitude toward me on K.'s part. I quickly became part of the small pantheon of psychic idols that helped him get through his days. He would often begin his session with a mantra that he repeated to himself countless times every day:

"Dr. G. was a second Sigmund Freud but Dr. Shengold is even better. I am a second Dr. Shengold! I am a second Dr. Shengold!"

Sometimes, under stress, he shouted this aloud—even when he was at work. (Incredibly enough, he had been able to find and keep a menial job among tolerant people, where he performed with a mechanical compliance and reliability that probably made him a valuable employee—or at least valuable enough to make his oddness tolerable.) Repeating the words that made him part of me and made me part of him seemed to help consolidate him, as it were. With this borrowed glue it was easier for him to make decisions as well as to ward off anxiety (as with the dangerous overexcitement in the toilet that I have described).

I do not think that K.'s staring at me in the elevator without apparent recall after he had left the treatment was either a conscious rejection or a reproachful rebuff. I was simply no longer recognized, having become part of the bad, useless, and relatively unavailable external world that generally corresponded only dimly to his inner registrations. My guess is that the "second Dr. Shengold" was still part of the array of prosthetic inner devices that crudely served K.'s mental life and sustained some sense of identity; but the Shengold crutch had been set aside in the service of K.'s need to share and borrow the available persona of his current therapist, thus becoming the "second Dr. X." The "second Dr.

Shengold" had now joined Dr. Freud and Dr. G. on the bench with the other seconds—fainter backup figures who had lost most of the clamorous, vital, magical power that can be conferred best by actual contact that promises the fulfillment of need.

K., the pathetic psychotic boy, shows in crude caricature something of what we all do in the course of meaningful emotional encounters with other people who register within our minds and modify preexistent registrations. He had retained into later life some of the myth-making intensity of the somatically and psychologically needy child's earliest relationships. These relationships with the earliest parental figures start with the parental bodily presence (characterized by psychoanalysts as the breast)[3]—a presence that is, I speculate, probably felt as part of the self whenever chaotic consciousness begins to occur. Freud characterizes this symbiosis of awakening awareness by imagining the infant as a kind of primal poet capable of saying, "'The breast is part of me, I am the breast,' [and] only later: 'I have it—that is, 'I am not it'" (1938, 299).

At first the separated other (which one can then have and no longer need be) exists only insofar as *it* fulfills a need. This first other, the object as distinct from the self, is an it since that which is separated out from the breast : me amalgam is conceived of by those speculating about the child's mind as a formerly self-part but now an other-part. As an entity now recognized as being outside the self, it has both animate (me) and thinglike (not me) qualities. It is a need-fulfilling, externalized body part (the parent reduced to a separated breast) and as such is not yet either a whole or a person (and so not yet *mother* or *father* or *she* or *he*). The whole person does not yet exist.[4]

At this early stage of the development of a separate identity, the child (like poor K.) needs actual, potentially need-satisfying contact to conceive of the existence of an (absolutely needed—see Faimberg 1991) other who can be counted on to reappear. K.'s identity-prostheses required a renewal of vitality that probably could be supplied only by the reliable geographic availability of the doctor, who was to be internalized as the good parent needed to feed and comfort and control him. K.'s inner images of the parental others had not

3. Cf. Philip Roth's novel *The Breast*.

4. Once, while visiting a psychiatric inpatient ward, I was approached by a patient I had never seen before—a drug addict—who greeted me as if I were some combination of lover, parent, and Messiah, passionately begging for medication with

yet attained enough of what Anna Freud calls "object constancy"—a lasting and dependable psychic picture which has become registered as part of the self and can be summoned up, even in the absence of the parent, to enable the child to postpone gratification and to control time and frustration by the work of his or her own mind—by active thought.[5]

The mind develops from origins that include one's own body and that of the first other; then its structure is enlarged and enriched by conjunction and identification with others. These contacts from later life borrow force and effect from the intensity and quality of the initial identificatory encounters. With the flourishing of thinking and the building up of an intellectual life, reading and hearsay make it possible to be influenced, sometimes profoundly, by those in whose physical presence one has not been—or even, if these are dead or from myth and story, those with whom one never can be. The later emotionally charged figures—such as teachers and other models—available for need-fulfillment, "love," emulation, and identification—not only derive their power from the earliest others but can and should modify those parts of the mind and self-image that are modeled on those primal connections.[6]

---

an emotional intensity that stemmed partly from his dramatic ability and partly from his pathetic need. When I told him I was not one of the ward doctors and had no power to help him, he suddenly became coldly expressionless, saying, "You don't exist!" This brought the psychoanalytic cliché *need-fulfilling object relationship* to experiential life for me.

5. Freud calls thought "trial action."

6. Freud (1923): "It is possible to suppose that the character of the ego [the 'I'] is a precipitate of abandoned object cathexes and that it contains the history of those object choices" (29).

2

FREUD'S EARLY LIFE AND FANTASIES

> In the course of his reprimand my father let
> fall the words: "The boy will come to nothing!"
> [Aus dem Buben wird nichts werden].
>
> Freud, *The Interpretation of Dreams*

"Sigmund Freud was born at 6:30 P.M. on the sixth of May, 1856, at 117 Schlossergasse, Freiburg, in Moravia"—thus begins Jones's great biography (1953, 1). Jones tells us *facts* about Freud's birth— we can be certain of them because others were there. Freud's mother experienced it; his father witnessed it.[1] But what does it mean to be born? None of us can recall it. Does being born mean to be nothing? or everything? We observe children and try to remember a beginning of awareness, but the subjectivity of infancy is beyond our grasp. We make do with guesses—many of them based on observations and speculations of the adult Sigmund Freud. Guesses or—better—fantasies; fantasies hedged by our observations, which are themselves hedged by transferences, projections, and fantasies.

One such fantasy comes from the playful mind of Samuel Butler. He envisioned a world of the souls of the Unborn. These souls speculate among themselves about what it means to be born:

> They have no knowledge, and cannot even conceive the existence of anything that is not such as they are themselves. Those who have been born are to them what the dead are to us. They can see no life in them, and know no more about them than they

---

1. Nevertheless, uncertainty about birth in relation to fathers is inescapable. Waelder (1960) criticizes "people . . . who request for every interpretation or proposition the kind of evidence we expect in the physical or chemical laboratory, i.e., evidence sufficiently conclusive to eliminate every possibility of doubt. With such requirements, of course, nobody could ever claim to be his father's issue" (4).

do of any stage in their own past development other than the one through which they are passing at the moment. They do not even know that their mothers are alive—much less that their mothers were once as they now are. To an embryo, its mother is simply the environment, and is looked upon much as our inorganic surroundings are by ourselves.

The great terror of their lives is the fear of birth,—that they shall have to leave the only thing that they can think of as life, and enter upon a dark unknown which is to them tantamount to annihilation.

Some, indeed, among them have maintained that birth is not the death which they commonly deem it, but that there is a life beyond the womb of which they as yet know nothing, and which is a million fold more truly life than anything they have yet been able even to imagine. But the greater number shake their yet unfashioned heads and say they have no evidence for this that will stand a moment's examination.

"Nay," answer the others, "so much work, so elaborate, so wondrous as that whereon we are now so busily engaged must have a purpose, though the purpose is beyond our grasp."

"Never," reply the first speakers; "our pleasure in the work is sufficient justification for it. Who has ever partaken of this life you speak of, and re-entered into the womb to tell us of it? Granted that some few have pretended to have done this, but how completely have their stories broken down when subjected to the tests of sober criticism? No. When we are born we are born, and there is an end of us." (1901, 491–92)

The playful and poetic mind can sometimes temper those who sound too sure of themselves with regard to continuing mysteries, like those of the beginning of our mental life. Psychoanalysts are supposed to be experts on what is known about the human mind. But how much have Freud and his followers added to the pittance supplied by artists and philosophers over the ages about birth and the beginning of awareness; and (the subject of Butler's parable) about death and the end of awareness? Freud's disciple Hanns Sachs said about the exploration of the mind by psychoanalysts, "Our deepest analyses are no more than scratching the surface with a harrow" (quoted by Gitelson 1973, 250). And Freud himself had the kind of mind that knows that defining and respecting what is not known are at least as important as determining what is.

This is a book about Sigmund Freud based in large part on how much we do not know and cannot know about him. The facts—observations by others and by Freud himself—have been gathered and interpreted memorably by Jones and (in our time) by Peter Gay and others. New facts may turn up. Perhaps we will come upon letters that will tell us "definitively" that Freud did or did not have an affair with his sister-in-law, or that she said they did, or that he said they didn't. Lies and distortions and gaps in our knowledge make such pieces of "historical truth" hard to establish.

There is no underestimating the importance of trying to establish the facts.[2] But Freud and those who followed his methods of investigation have found that to know a human being one must above all know, as far as one can know, the nature and content of his or her fantasies, the dynamic central core of the life of the mind. (This is the message of so many papers by Jacob Arlow.) Those fantasies are both conscious and unconscious and dynamically involved in conflictual transformations and regressions. They are products not only of what we think and feel as adults (when thinking is predominantly rational and ruled by what Freud [1900b] calls "secondary process") but also of the way we think and feel as children (dominated by the primary process of the primitive mind). Here is something that we do know is generally true; we also know how difficult it is to bring our fantasies to full consciousness and, especially, to own them (to feel them more than intellectually and acknowledge them with responsibility and conviction). Simply to get full and coherent accounts of our fantasies means working against all sorts of inner resistances. Some fantasies, Freud says, are universal. But this is true in the sense that all human beings have

2. Freud would have hated this enterprise in relation to himself. Jones (1953) quotes a letter Freud wrote to his fiancée, Martha Bernays, when he was twenty-eight: "I have just carried out one resolution which one group of people, as yet unborn and fated to misfortune, will feel acutely . . . they are my biographers. I have destroyed all my diaries of the past fourteen years, with letters, scientific notes and the manuscripts of my publications. . . . The stuff simply enveloped me, as the sand does the Sphinx, and soon only my nostrils would show above the mass of paper. I cannot leave here and I cannot die before ridding myself of the disturbing thought of who might come by the old papers. . . . Let the biographers chafe; we won't make it too easy for them. Let each of them believe he is right in this 'Conception of the Development of the Hero': even now I enjoy the thought of how they will all go astray" (xii–xiii). Freud already saw himself as a Hero—and one who might, like Oedipus, have to face the Sphinx and face the danger of being smothered by her.

faces with eyes, nose, mouth, ears, and so on. Each person has an individual set of variable combinations of the universal fantasies, and, like facial features, no two are quite the same. To state that Freud had preoedipal and oedipal conflicts and complexes is to deprive him of his individuality; some psychobiographers treat these obvious facts as if they had made a valuable discovery about their subject.

Freud has shown us how many of our fantasies, how many of our internal pictures of the world on which our fantasies are based, are formed in relation to our parents. We take them and their attitudes toward past and present culture into our minds in the course of fashioning our own psychic structure, functioning, and temperament.

Freud, like all of us, would initially have felt that They (the parents, who are probably first registered as godlike primal parents) are right and know everything. Although he was born with a caul and became the focus of all sorts of magical expectations and intense attentions as his young mother's first child and son, his disillusion with authority and his parents must have begun early, as it does for us all, and continued intermittently.

Freud has recorded one of the early climactic experiences of disillusion:

> One evening before going to sleep I disregarded the rules which modesty lays down and obeyed the call of nature in my parents' bedroom while they were present. In the course of his reprimand my father let fall the words: "The boy will come to nothing!" (1900a, 221). This must have been a frightful blow to my ambition, for references to this scene are still constantly recurring in my dreams and are always linked with an enumeration of my achievements and successes, as though I wanted to say: "You see, I have come to something!" (Freud 1900b, 216)

Freud wrote this in his masterpiece, *The Interpretation of Dreams*. In the third English edition of that book (1932) he inserted a comment that could be read as stating—or assuming—"You see [Father], I *have* come to something":

> This book, with the new contribution to psychology which *surprised the world* when it was published (1900), remains essentially unaltered. It contains, even according to my present-day judgment [this was 1931, when Freud was seventy-five] the most

valuable of all the *discoveries* it has been my good fortune to make. *Insight such as this falls to one's lot but once in a lifetime.* (1900b, xxxii; my italics)

The old man, a discoverer who, like Copernicus and Darwin, has challenged and conquered the world and is now a *conquistador,* successful and famous, can hold up this piece of insight to show father how far "the boy" has come.[3]

It is easy to see how the boy would recoil from his father in ambivalent conflict—wanting to get rid of the beloved and needed one who could so humiliate him, mortify his narcissism, thwart his sexual and ambitious wishes, and threaten him with all the psycho-logical dangers that could be condensed in the terrible prophetic word *nothing.* It is easy to see how readily he would try to find other parental figures to identify with or other selves who had become something with the aid of—even in defiance of—other fathers and mothers: like Abraham and Joseph in the Bible, great ones like Hannibal or Napoleon, who had gone further than their fathers would have ventured, fictional characters like Gargantua and Gulliver, who as giants have little need for parents. (Freud said, in relation to his experience of estrangement when he first climbed the Acropolis, "It seems as though the essence of success was to have got further than one's father, and as though to excel one's father was still something forbidden" [1936, 247].)

People in his life, father figures (Freud kept away from aware-ness of the perhaps even more important mothers) like his teachers "the great Brücke" (1900a, 290) and Josef Breuer, would capture not only the ambivalent conflict involving Jacob Freud but also the mythical and historical reworked editions (revenants with a differ-ence) of him. Freud, constantly remolding his inner images of parents that were malleable parts of himself, would find these reworkings evoked by and projected onto other men: sometimes younger men who could also transiently be brothers and sons. (Mother and sisters were of course at least equally involved, but more covertly.) An extraordinary condensation of all this was con-centrated on his friend Wilhelm Fliess, somewhat lessened in rela-

3. I have elsewhere (1991) connected the well-known statement about insight with Freud's use of the dream "Father, don't you see I'm burning?" in the Dream book—stressing the importance in that book and in Freud's work in general of metaphors involving fire, light, travel, and sight—all linked with Freud's ambition and need to *show* his father how far from "nothing" the boy had come.

tion to Carl Jung, still significant but further reduced when brought to Karl Abraham. And there were of course many other relatives, friends, colleagues, and acquaintances who were at least fleetingly involved in Freud's kaleidoscopic identities.

For Freud as for any educated person, the assimilable others included characters from literature. Goethe's *Sorrows of Young Werther* pushed a whole generation of young people toward suicide. And think of the influence on Freud of Oedipus and Hamlet. Freud, in turn, remade Oedipus and Hamlet partly in his own image and has influenced subsequent readers with Freud's Oedipus and Freud's Hamlet.[4] Primo Levi had something characteristically marvelous to say about this soul-shaping power of fiction, speaking partly as a reader but primarily from the point of view of the creative novelist looking at his characters and where they came from:

> Every one of these phantasms is born from you, has your blood, for good or evil. It is your bloom. Worse, it is a spy assigned to you, reveals a part of you, your tensions, like those glass tassels that are used to reveal whether a crack in the wall is bound to grow wider. They are your way of saying "I": when you make them move or speak, reflect on what you are doing for they might say too much. Perhaps they will live longer than you, perpetuating your vices and errors.
>
> The characters of a book are in truth strange creatures. They have neither skin nor blood nor flesh, they have less reality than a painting or a nocturnal dream, they have no substance but words, black doodles on a white sheet of paper, and yet you pass the time with them, converse with them through the centuries, fall in love with them. . . . Just as it is impossible to transform a real person into a character, that is, fashion an objective undistorted biography of him, so it is impossible to perform the reverse operation, to coin a character without pouring into it not only your moods as the author but also fragments of people you have met or of other characters. (Levi 1985, 118–19)

We use such fragments for our self-images as well as for our images of others (our self and object representations, which, aside from their changeability, have close resemblances to fictional characters).

Freud said that he was a good hater. He had to deal with the

---

4. Similarly James Joyce digested and refashioned Ulysses.

great dilemma that is part of the human condition, part of an inexorable trap that starts even in the narcissistic period of development, when our claim to self-sufficiency and omnipotence is pitifully dependent on the ministrations of another: we are driven to get rid of the very others we cannot live without. What are we to do with our murderous impulses? Here is where expendable others are needed as scapegoats on which to discharge our hatred.

There was an alternation between idealization and hatred worked out in part in the long, conflicted, and emotionally passionate relationship with Fliess that accompanied the most intense part of Freud's self-analysis. He obviously learned something from that experience, although he was not able to transcend it fully. His ambivalence toward Fliess, his greatest friend-who-became-an-enemy (which had its antecedents in his relation to his parents, his half-brothers, his siblings, and his nephew John), was repeated in his life perhaps most markedly in relation to Jung; and hatred continued to erupt briefly, especially in regard to son-figures, like Tausk, Rank, Ferenczi, and Abraham. (And most of these relationships had bad, Fliess-like endings.) But after Fliess, despite oedipal rivalries and the revival of masochistic and passive homosexual wishes of considerable power (evidenced by his fainting fits—see below), he had an overall ability to contain his hatred, to turn it outward toward others with relative appropriateness and to control the turning of destructiveness inward upon himself. He certainly seemed able to maintain his considerable self-esteem.[5]

It was easier for Freud (as it is for almost everyone) to shift many of his conflicted feelings away from the "parents" and "siblings" and "children" in the flesh to great minds of the past. They are more readily idealized and as such fulfill all sorts of needs; but, perhaps more important, they are safer from the intensities of murderous hatred that fuel all the psychological situations of danger. The great ones are no longer vulnerable; we cannot lose them since they belong to eternity. Above all, we cannot actually kill them since they are already dead or have never lived. In our minds ("thinking is trial action") we can play with solving the impossible dilemma: we can—with relative impunity—both kill them off and

5. We know too little about the complex relationship of the mind to physical illness to be able to determine how much Freud's developing the cancer of the mouth that led to his death in old age had some powerful basis in transformed *psychological* self-destructiveness.

keep them forever. We can identify with them and, mentally, kill off *their* enemies, hate *their* parents. We can cannibalize them and make them part of ourselves without harm or loss. Getting away from the primal figures (usually the mother) so heavily invested in narcissistic need and dangerous conflicts in our minds (and so vulnerable in the flesh) to others, and especially to historical and fictional others, permits us a wonderful and potentially playful flexibility. (Or at least it permits approaching this at times.) The need for deadening defenses is lessened; murder and incest, death and loss can be safely distanced for a while; flexibility and play can make room for work and for love.

3

THE EGO IDEAL

To have firmly established . . . that in the light of
psychoanalysis, moral valuation and moral conduct
are necessary attributes of "natural man". . . is perhaps the most important contribution Freud has
made to the study of moral behavior.

H. Hartmann, *Psychoanalysis and Moral Values*

Psychoanalysts have various ways of trying to picture the emer-
gence of a separate identity from the original mother/child unit,
but all our theoretical terms are metaphors for a most complicated
developmental process that seems to take place (past an unknown
and probably unknowable period of inborn maturation) mainly by
the infant's taking into its separating mind aspects of the parental
people who care for her or him. At the beginning of our existence,
we absolutely need other people; but to be able to develop on our
own we have to identify with those people—register them in our
minds—and learn to care for, to mother, ourselves. To achieve
autonomy, we need psychologically to become our own parents.

The psychic impact of one person upon another cannot be
simple and straightforward. The mind, once past its undiscoverable
subjective beginning (and undoubtedly not even then), is not tabula
rasa. We bring less with us into the world that is perfected than
other species do, but the individually varying sum of the potentials
we bring is so considerable and so mysterious. (Human beings are
born unequal; equality at birth is there only in a theoretical, potential, and moral sense: we deserve to be treated as if we are born
equal.) We have somehow to take into our minds aspects of those
who feed and care for us in order eventually to attain the powers
and the mastery of reality of the mothering (and later the father-
ing) figure. Infants do this somehow—in part initially by becoming
like (identifying with) the person and later on the people who

surround them and take care of them. Still later, the young child also responds when (by now meaningful) people are lost or felt as lost (or when primitive registrations of those people are, at least to a considerable extent, given up) by becoming like them. These massive and partial "identifications" are superimposed on some inborn maturational schemata of separate mental development.

These depositions of others and parts of others within the mind to become part of the self are probably gross and diffuse at first, and the way we identify evolves to become more selective and discriminatory (as part of development from primitive to mature psychic functioning). What is taken in from others is usually (and, with maturation, increasingly) distorted and transformed. It is probably never simple duplication—in part at first because of what is psychically there prior to superimposed identifications as the result of inborn genetic differences. After the earliest developmental period—that is, after the psychologically complex evolving of separateness and identity—the effects of subsequent identifications are less profound and less discernable (but not always less important) than the original primary ones that they modify.

We are psychic carriers of the past; we are both trapped and enriched by this. Still there remains some capacity for transformation and novelty. There are inborn evolutionary patterns—probably for identification itself, for instance. In later development, we look for, expect to find, and (realistically or in fantasy) "see" in other people aspects of what we have identified with in our earliest parental contacts (transference); and we also externalize onto others aspects of what we have become and are (projection). Primitive functioning of these mechanisms becomes more discriminating and modifiable as the child matures and achieves a separate identity. Evidence of both unconscious and conscious *will* gradually appears, some proportion of which is at least felt as free.

Our initial wishes for everything, our views of ourselves and our parents as everything, become progressively modified but are never completely lost. It is not only the effect of parental warnings, like that of Freud's father's dire prediction about his naughty young child's future, but also part of our human nature that makes it inevitable that everyone ("the girl" as well as "the boy") wants to come to everything. We are constantly seeking more than we can get, expecting more than others can supply, alongside—past the shock of the first experiences of pain (and what Freud calls "unpleasure")—looking to avoid something. Because of our (evolving) inborn instinctual nature (always modified by the environment), we develop a number of specific (evolving) instinctual needs; these inevitably activate a number of (evolving) danger situations, and these, in turn, require psychic defenses which also become more complicated as we mature. What emerges is continuous but varying intrapsychic conflict. The mind is additionally burdened with a compulsion to repeat the past, and a compulsion to get away from the compulsion to repeat the past.

Because human beings are subject to a biologically imposed long period of maturation requiring dependence, all of us start merged with a parent (possessing, as it were, a parental incubus-and-succubus). This is the intensely powerful beginning of our continuing overall need for another without whom initially we cannot survive (and later, without whom we are disposed to feel we cannot survive). But most of us have enough inborn equipment and receive enough sustaining care to develop considerable ability to distance and dilute our continuing dependent needs, although these never disappear and can regain their power in regressive situations. The separation occurs as part of needing to and being able to grasp the exigencies and frustrations imposed by external and internal reality, especially the inevitability of our death and our parents' deaths and of our species' diminished and precarious place in the universe. We must leave the Garden of Eden with its promise of immortality and bliss, but that permits us a considerable measure of individuality and our own humanity. We experience in our early development a transient, tragically imperfect, constantly dissolving godhood. The promise of paradise is lost, but we retain what Wordsworth calls "intimations": the need and the power to idealize, which can in some measure transform reality. We gradually and reluctantly give up omniscience and grandiosity, but we can, at least intermittently, make life precious by learning to value, care for, and love ourselves, our children, one another, our causes. We can "come to something."

Psychoanalysts speak of the self, of the ego (the sense of I), of a differentiated part of the ego involved with morality called the superego, of a differentiated part of the superego called the ego ideal. There is an arbitrariness about the definitions of these subjective entities in psychoanalysis, inevitable when dealing with the ineffable and the unknown, that can be confusing. Perhaps this confusion is justifiable; it does indicate how much uncertainty there is about these phenomena. But there is general agreement that both the ego and the superego derive from what arises in the developmental course of drive gratification—the first steps in what we clumsily call object relations (the evolving ability to deal with other people): the internalization of others to form and modify the structure and image of the self, first of the parents—with subsequent supplementation and tempering by becoming like important other people (see Arlow 1989).

The superego, which is a differentiated part of the ego, the mind's hypothetical moral agency according to Freud, specifically develops out of identifications with parental controlling attitudes: parental prohibitions and parental caring.[1] What the parents do and do not do externally to manage the child is taken in, not without alterations and distortions, to form an internal controlling moral system. This part of the mind begins to have its secure although still developing substance and structure (independent of the earlier external parental influences, which still continue to affect the mind) as an outcome of the partial and provisional (but consequential) moral system formation (superego formation) at the time of the "resolution" of the Oedipus complex. The instinctual wishes toward the parents are altered enough to make for a considerable giving up of the parents as the fulfillers of one's wishes and the centers of the instinctual primitive world. This loss, in Freud's view, contributes definitively to superego formation. There is subsequent continuing modification. Hartmann says,

> [There is a] long way . . . from the interiorization of parental demands after the [time of the] oedipal conflicts to the more elaborate moral codes of the adult. (1960, 31)

The continuation of the instinctual drives (sexual and aggressive, to have sex and to murder) as well as the change in external forces which impinge on the moral system makes regression a constant possibility.

> The "moral system" of the individual [can be] imperiled by the economy of the instinctual drives, in a more specific sense perhaps mostly by the aggressive drive. An imbalance can occur because, as Freud discovered, contrary to expectation, the check-

1. Hartmann: "Not only the prohibitions of the parents, but also their love survives in the relationship of the superego to the ego" (1960, 27).

ing of aggression can make a person's superego more tyrannical [leading to an increase in the need for punishment]. (Hartmann 1960, 29)

This statement underlines the complexity of the internalization of parental qualities—the result is far more than a simple mirroring imitation. In evaluating the role of the moral system in the adult's mental health and its resistance to regression, Hartmann stresses the optimal eventual developmental attainment of stability, autonomy, and especially integrative power. (For Hartmann, the functioning of the moral system involves both ego and superego components—see 1960, 29.)

The moral system both threatens and encourages—employs both the stick and the carrot. In current psychoanalytic theory the punitive aspect of the moral system is considered a prime function of the superego; the accompanying influence of the good in directing behavior is held to be a function of that part of the superego now called the ego ideal.

It can be confusing that when Freud introduced the term *ego ideal* in 1914, he used it as a preliminary label for the entire mental structure envisioned as performing the critical function of a moral psychic agency; this later became the superego in his hypothetical tripartite structure of the mental apparatus. After 1914, the connotations of the ego ideal in Freud's writings and in those of his followers changed. In the structural metaphor currently used in psychoanalysis, the ego ideal is generally regarded as a specific part or aspect of the superego (an inner, transformed, structured registration of the watchdog functions of the parents), although some prefer to consider it a separate entity. The ego ideal's operations are seen as benevolent, aiming toward the promise of the good, beckoning reward; this is in contrast to the conscience function of the superego, which provides censorship and threatens punishment. Both sets of functions have an evolution, with early primitive structures continuing to exist alongside more mature and developed ones; as always in mental life, primitive functioning can take over with regression.

Here I am not attempting a full historical review (see the excellent one by Sandler et al. 1963) or a precise definition or a complete developmental outline of the ego ideal. I am trying to understand the individual's pursuit of an ideal based on having received praise and love and on a continuing search for praise and love—an ideal that would appear to become a part of his or her mental apparatus. This psychic formation begins with the original narcissistic promises of glory and omnipotence that color the nearly absolute dependency that marks early mental life. The initial feeling of centrality can promise wonderful fulfillment, and the positive side of feeling so important can also be used defensively, to avoid and deny the *bad* (that which evokes the psychical situations of danger). Early representations of both the self and the object are idealized. Idealization is needed and used to counter devaluation (the reduction from feeling oneself as everything toward feeling oneself as nothing). Idealization and devaluation can be regarded as primary defensive and expressive modes of the ego itself. Most analysts, probably wisely, follow Freud's model of the mind, somewhat arbitrarily viewing the superego as a specific structure separate from the ego out of which it develops. But Freud also describes it as a specialized part of the ego: "a critical agency within the ego, which even in normal times takes up a critical attitude toward the ego itself" (1921, 109).[2]

In his shifting views of the ego ideal, Freud consistently regarded it as the heir of narcissism. In 1914, he writes of the individual's projecting his initial narcissism "onto this new ego ideal . . . [which becomes] the substitute for the lost narcissism of his childhood in which he was his own ideal" (94). In the *New Introductory Lectures* of 1933, Freud, now describing the superego as "the vehicle for the ego ideal," adds,

> There is no doubt that this ego ideal is the precipitate of the old picture of the parents, the expression of admiration for the perfection which the child then attached to them. (64–65)

If we combine the two we see that Freud is talking about the ego ideal as deriving from the child's grandiose, "good" representations both of the self and of the parents, representations that are evolving in the early narcissistic developmental period of mental life. It functions as heir to the narcissistic omnipotence granted by the child to both partners in the original narcissistic dyad: the idealized

2. We are after all dealing with *metaphors* of structure—a model, not anything as concrete and inexorable as *actual* (anatomical) structure. It cannot ever be perfectly "right." The justification for keeping Freud's structural hypothesis of the mental apparatus (id, ego, superego) is its heuristic usefulness.

self and the idealized parent (Kohut's "grandiose self" and "idealized object").[3]

From these narcissistic beginnings (which add to and modify unknown givens and maturational factors already present at birth), the ego ideal (like the superego, like the ego itself) is modified by way of additional, later, and progressively less narcissistic identifications with the parents. (The identifications constantly interplay with projections onto the parents.) To form this dynamic ego ideal each of us takes into our mind our often far-from-objective registrations or representations of parental points of view; of social, moral, and cultural attitudes as transmitted by and embodied in the parents. From childhood on, additions and modifications are derived from the people who supplement the primary parental figures as meaningful others in the course of the individual's development: nurses, grandparents, siblings, governesses, teachers, doctors, political and cultural leaders (past and present), friends, lovers, psychoanalysts, and so forth. Starting with the internalized primal parent from the earliest period of mental life (a figure whose registration Freud views as beginning with the parent as part of the self), the child can project onto other currently actual or historical or fictional persons who operate as alter egos or "ego ideal figures," tempering the already internalized aspects of the idealized self and of the idealized parents. Subsequently these ego ideal figures, now within the mind, can be, in assimilated and modified form, further projected onto substitutes for family figures (Carl Jung or Karl Abraham could for Freud evoke his mental registration of Wilhelm Fliess, who had previously evoked the registrations of father, mother, siblings, and so on).

We constantly change the cast in the theater of our minds but always retain the old figures alongside and underneath the new. We thus continually make use of our maturing life experience and contacts to repopulate and also, in varying degree, to modify the existing characters of our inner world; figures that we make use of as working parts of our self, like the second Dr. Shengold / I that became a prosthesis of the patient I discussed in chapter 1. The new figures can change us, but much, of course most, remains as before. The substitutes can reproduce the full effects evoked by the originals or can represent attenuated versions (for Freud, Jung

3. Sandler et al., 1963: The ego ideal includes "both ideal object and ideal self representations" (83).

was easier to deal with than Fliess). The most malleable ego ideal figures, the least vulnerable to loss and destruction, and felt as the least dangerous are usually those who are dead or derived from history, fiction, and myth; despite the transference and projection onto them of primal intensities, their distance makes them the safest.

Freud's postulated psychic structures (id, ego, superego, ego ideal) are part of psychoanalytic theoretical *metaphor,* a way of thinking about certain functions of the mind rather than structural entities that have a real existence. There is a certain capriciousness in separating the superego from the ego, the ego ideal from the superego, and differences of opinion about definition, so common in psychoanalytic literature, are in this instance no sin; they do not concern fixed scientific fact inexorably determined by external reality. We are dealing not so much with separate parts of the mind (although this is our theoretical picture) as with separate psychic functions. Some of these functions appear in our consciousness only when the mind is in conflict within itself. In ordinary, relatively conflict-free functioning, the roles we assign to the superego and the ego ideal are performed in a fashion that does not necessarily make their separation discernable (an observation emphasized by Beres 1958). In the absence of apparent conflict (theoretically there would always be some below consciousness) or the close scrutiny that may come from clinical psychoanalysis or gifted and expert self-observation, ordinary functioning does not give rise to anxious or painful awareness of part of the self divided off from another part of the self.

I can illustrate this complexity by quoting from Proust. No one is better than Marcel Proust at transcribing and describing the creative, transient, and above all dynamically complicated amalgam (a product of the past and the present) that makes up a person's identity of the moment. He illustrates how we make use of others in this regard, metabolizing them and blending them in our adaptive attitudes toward new relationships which repeat and transmute old ones. In the following excerpt from *Remembrance of Things Past,* the narrator, Marcel, speaks tenderly and sensually with his mistress, Albertine. The exchange that elicits Proust's psychological observation starts, significantly enough, with a goodnight kiss. It is the description of the suffering of the child Marcel missing his mother's goodnight kiss that begins Proust's gigantic novel. The finally administered maternal kiss portrays Marcel's mother's overindulgence in the face of his separation anxiety—the beginning of the path, in Proust's opinion, to his namesake hero's—and the author's—oedipally charged neurosis.

> When it was Albertine's turn to bid me goodnight, kissing me on either side of my neck, her hair caressed me like a wing of softly bristling feathers. Incomparable as were those two kisses of peace, Albertine slipped into my mouth, in making me the gift of her tongue, as it were a gift of the Holy Ghost, conveyed to me a viaticum, left me with a provision of tranquillity almost as precious as when my mother in the evening at Combray used to lay her lips upon my forehead.
>
> "Are you coming with us tomorrow, old crosspatch?" she would ask before leaving me. "Where are you going?"
>
> "That will depend on the weather and on you. But have you written anything today, my little darling? . . . Tell me, by the way, when I came in this evening, you knew my step, you guessed at once who it was?"
>
> "Of course. Could I possibly be mistaken? Couldn't I tell my little sparrow's hop among a thousand? She must let me take her shoes off before she goes to bed, it will give me such pleasure. You're so nice and pink in all that white lace." (72)

The narrator then realizes, on examining the language he has been using in addressing his mistress, that some of his attitudes, wishes, and verbal expressions are derived from figures from his past—grandmother, parents, other relatives, even from his own past self:

> Such was my answer [to Albertine]; amid the sensual expressions, others will be recognized that were peculiar to my grandmother and my mother. For, little by little, I was beginning to resemble all my relations: my father who—in a very different fashion from myself, no doubt, *for if things repeat themselves, it is with great variations*—took so keen an interest in the weather; and not my father only, but, more and more, my Aunt Léonie. . . . And as if it were not enough that I bear an exaggerated resemblance to my father, to the extent of not being satisfied like him with consulting the barometer, but becoming an animated barometer myself, as if it were not enough that I should allow myself to be ordered by my Aunt Léonie to stay at home to watch the weather, from my bedroom and even from my bed, here I was talking now to Albertine, at one moment as the child that I

had been at Combray used to talk to my mother, at another as my grandmother used to talk to me. When we have passed a certain age, the soul of the child that we were and the souls of the dead from whom we sprang come and shower upon us their riches and their spells, asking to be allowed to contribute to the new emotions which we feel and in which, erasing their former image, we recast them in an original creation. Thus my whole past from my earliest years, and, beyond this, the past of my parents and relations, blended with my impure love for Albertine the tender charm of an affection at once filial and maternal. We have to give hospitality, at a certain stage in our lives, to all our relatives who have journeyed so far and gathered round us. (1923, 72–74; my italics)[4]

This marvelous expression of the shifting complexity of human identity in which the present is creatively derived from the past (and the self from others) shows, better than any clinical description I know, how difficult it is to separate out our theoretically derived psychic structures like the ego, the superego, the ego ideal; and how complicated and dynamic are our easily oversimplified concepts of mental representations of the self and of others. Surely we are nearer the experiential "truth" in viewing our ideas of the mind as collections of functions rather than structures. Our psychoanalytic metaphor of psychic structures remains useful but should be used with modesty and not too much insistence on exact, "scientific" definition.

4. Warren Poland, when this book was in press, published an article (1992)—written long before he had read any part of my manuscript—in which he made use of part of the same passage from Proust to illustrate some of his ideas about transference. Almost incredibly, out of all of the thousands of pages of Proust's great novel, we had both seized on the same few pages to illustrate our ideas.

4

BIBLICAL HEROES I:
JOSEPH AND FREUD

> What Freud teaches is the freedom of interpreta-
> tion, even though he himself was perhaps the most
> tendentious interpreter in all of Western intellec-
> tual tradition. His most Jewish quality was his deep
> conviction that there is sense in everything, and
> that such meaning could be brought up to the
> light. He read the unconscious as Judaic exegesis
> read the Hebrew Bible, with every nuance, every
> omission, being made to show an extraordinary
> wealth of significance.
>
> —H. Bloom, Foreword to Ken Frieden, *Freud's*
> *Dream of Interpretation*[1]

After reading Thomas Mann's *Joseph in Egypt* (1938), Freud wrote
the author,

> I keep wondering if there isn't a figure in history for whom
> the life of Joseph was a mythical prototype, allowing us to detect
> the phantasy of Joseph as the secret daemonic motor behind the
> scenes of his complex life. I am thinking of Napoleon I. (Freud
> 1960, 432)

What Freud goes on to say of Napoleon as Joseph, and of
Napoleon's relation to his older brother, Joseph, provides a fasci-

---

1. Bloom writes this in his foreword to Ken Frieden's (1990) book *Freud's Dream
of Interpretation*, which convincingly connects with Judaic dream interpretations
which Freud rejected out of "his wish to sever all ties between himself and ancient
dream interpreters" (Frieden 1990, xi). Frieden contends that Freud's rejection of
linking his ideas with biblical and talmudic dream interpretation was *denial* in the
psychoanalytic sense.

nating way of looking at the emperor: examining Napoleon's transferences and identifications in relation to a mythical figure. But
Freud himself lived out a Joseph fantasy.

Mann, in his essay on Freud, agrees with and quotes "a Viennese
scholar of the Freudian school" (it was Ernst Kris) who spelled out
the "fundamental motif" in Mann's Joseph novels (1934, 1936) of
an individual living out the life of a mythical character type: "pre-
cisely this idea of the 'lived life,' life as succession, as a moving in
other's steps, as identification" (Mann 1936, 24–25) with figures
from the past. In previous chapters I outlined a similar concept of
making use of great men and women from myth and history to act
as spiritual fathers and mothers, brothers and sisters, and as alter-
native selves in the service of the formation of the superego and
of ego ideals: the parental figures and the culture from the past
made part of the mind and self.

Freud presents himself as Joseph for the first time in *The Interpretation of Dreams* (1900). There he documents his involvement
with the biblical Joseph and "other people of that name":

> It will be noticed that the name Josef plays a great part in my
> dreams (cf. the dream about my uncle). My own ego finds it very
> easy to hide itself behind people of that name, since Joseph was
> the name of a man famous in the Bible as an interpreter of
> dreams. (484)

But Freud's interest in biblical heroes had started much earlier, and
in his *Autobiographical Study* (1925) he mentions this as a determi-
nant of his curiosity about human beings and his ultimate choice
of a life's work:

> My deep engrossment in the Bible story (almost as soon as I
> had learnt the art of reading) had, as I recognized much later,
> an enduring effect upon the direction of my interest. (8)

Even earlier, his Catholic nurse, whom he called the primary orig-
inator of his neurosis, had deeply impressed him with her stories
about God and hell.

Freud's specific interest in the biblical tale of Joseph, son of
Jacob, must have been very great when he was a child since it
reflected his own family situation (see Eissler 1963, 1104). Similarity
and identity of names always impressed Freud. His own father's
name was Jacob [*Jakob*], and this Jacob too had had two wives.
(Actually Freud's father had three, but it is not known if Sigmund

was aware of the second wife.) Sigmund, like Joseph, was the eldest child of the beloved younger wife. Jacob Freud was born in 1815 and married when he was seventeen. His first son, Emmanuel (father of Freud's childhood companion John), was born in 1832 or 1833. His second son, Phillip, was born in 1836. Jacob Freud married again when he was forty. He and Amalie Nathanson (*his* Rachel) had eight children. Sigmund was the eldest, born twenty years after his half-brother, Phillip; then, a little less than a year later, came Julius, who died at eight months. Ten years after Sigmund, the youngest, Alexander, was born. In between were five girls.

Jones (1953) describes how Freud's unusual family constellation incited his curiosity and facilitated his later discovery of the universality of the Oedipus complex. The relations of the hero to father and brothers (with concomitant relations to mother and sisters) in the Joseph story parallel those in Sigmund's family. Joseph was the favorite son, not only of the doting Rachel, but also of Jacob, who had eleven other children. Sigmund was Jacob's pride and joy and was, of course, the firstborn and lifelong favorite of his mother (cf. Goethe, see chapter 7 below).

Freud was ambitious (he called himself a conquistador, a conqueror), and in his paper on Goethe he links, as the natural heritage of a gifted, indisputable family favorite, confidence and ambition. This combination is young Joseph's strength as well as the sin that led him to the pit; and it is attested to by Joseph's dreams. He dreams first that his sheaf stands up and remains upright while those of his brothers gather around and bow low to it; then he dreams that the sun, the moon, and eleven stars bow down to him. The first dream is of phallic ascendancy over his brothers—to be first in the eyes of the parents.[2]

Joseph's second dream has him also ruling over his parents. Jacob reproaches him, "Are we to come, I and your mother and your brothers, and bow low to you to the ground?" (Gen. 37:10). Joseph's brothers are infuriated by his dreams. Freud (1900) writes of his own fraternal rivalries. We learn most about his relations with his much older half-brother Phillip; his younger brother Julius, who lived such a short time; his nephew John, who was a year older

---

2. Zeligs (1955) interprets these dreams of ambition as defensive—the greatness compensatory to the feelings of the weaker young brother vis-à-vis his hostile, stronger older brothers.

than Sigmund. Phillip was old enough to be—and was confused with—his father; John's role was that of an older brother. We read of Freud's warm and loving feeling toward the ten-year-younger Alexander (Sigmund's Benjamin).

If, as Freud hypothesizes, and work with patients suggests, the primal crime (as registered in the superego) is parricide,[3] the biblical myth portrays a displacement in the murder of Abel by Cain. The father is defied in the eating of the forbidden fruit, but the first murder is that of brother by brother, out of jealousy for the father's love: "The Lord paid heed to Abel and his offering, but to Cain and his offering he paid no heed" (Gen. 37:3,4).

Genesis is full of stories of hatred and rivalry between brothers—Cain and Abel, Isaac and Ishmael, Esau and Jacob. In every instance the father is spared, and rage is turned against the brother. Jacob, with the connivance of his mother, Rebekah, steals his older brother's birthright and his blessing by trickery. The paternal blessing not only passes on the goods and power of the father but also confers the privilege of carrying on the Covenant with God—that special relationship with God the Father (the primal parent) which led the envious Cain to murder Abel. It is largely the not-unwarranted expectation that Joseph will be the recipient of Jacob's blessing that rouses the older brothers' hatred and fear of the young boy.[4] Reuben, the eldest and the natural heir (as was Esau), had offended against his father by seducing Jacob's favorite concubine, Bilhah. Mann portrays Reuben as partly motivated toward the incest by his jealous rage at the prospect that the young Joseph (then seven) would be preferred over him.

It is when Joseph is seventeen, following the telling of his overweening dreams, that the brothers resolve to kill him, thereby also venting their fury against their father. Joseph is first cast down into the pit and then, Reuben having managed to dissuade those more zealous for murder, is sold into slavery. He again descends—to Egypt, which Mann calls hell or the lower world. He rises by

---

3. "If the Son of God was obliged to sacrifice his life to redeem mankind from original sin, then by the law of talion, . . . that sin must have been a killing, a murder. . . . And [if] the original sin was an offense against God the Father, [then] the primal crime of mankind must have been a parricide, the killing of the primal father of the primitive human horde, whose mnemic image was later transfigured into a deity" (Freud 1915, 292–93).

4. The rivalry of Jung and Abraham was certainly in part over the wish to be Freud's favorite and his heir—as it were, for his blessing.

becoming the steward of Potiphar and again is cast down—this time into prison—because of the accusation of Potiphar's wife. His power of dream interpretation enables him to rise again. He gains Pharaoh's trust and becomes his first minister—the highest in all the land, save Pharaoh himself.[5] Joseph, through leaving his father and transcending his dependency on him, finally attains a position from which he can father his father and his brothers.

The displacement from father-murder to brother-murder is also seen in *Hamlet,* where Claudius says of his crime,

> O, my offense is rank, it smells to heaven.
> It hath the primal eldest curse upon't
> A brother's murder. (III.iii.36–38)

In Freud's view, the play hinges on the murderous (and incestuous) wishes toward his father (and mother) that paralyze Hamlet; he cannot kill the brother of his father who acted out what Hamlet himself desired to do. Freud comments on this in a momentous letter to Fliess announcing his discovery of the Oedipus complex, and in so doing he provides, by way of a slip, the counterpart of his own father-to-brother displacement. It is the letter of October 15, 1897, written a year after his father's death had launched Freud on the great task of self-analysis. Hamlet, Freud (1954) says, hesitates to avenge his father because of his unconscious feeling of guilt, for he himself "had meditated the same deed against his father from passion for his mother" (266). It is not characteristic of Hamlet, Freud adds, to avoid aggressive action, considering that

> he is the same man who sends his courtiers to their deaths without a scruple, and who is positively precipitate in killing Laertes. (1954, 266)

Hamlet is not "precipitate" in killing Laertes; he does so unwittingly, having no knowledge of the poison that makes his slight scratching of Laertes fatal. But he does precipitately kill Polonius,[6] the father of Laertes, whom he hears behind the arras in his

---

5. The descents and ascents, from the lower regions to the upper world, are reminiscent of Freud's imagery in *The Interpretation of Dreams* (see Shengold 1966). The epigraph of the Dream book is "Flectere si nequeo superos, Acheronta movebo" (ix) (If I cannot bend the higher powers, I shall move the lower regions)—the motto of a conquistador.

6. Hamlet's precipitate murderous action is underlined by his accompanying

mother's bedchamber and mistakes for his uncle ("I took thee for thy better" [II.iv.34]).

Freud repeated this observation (without the error) in a parallel passage in the Dream book (1900):

Hamlet is far from being represented as a person incapable of taking any action. We see him doing so on two occasions: first in a sudden outburst of temper, when he runs his sword through the eavesdropper behind the arras, and secondly in a premeditated and even crafty fashion, when, with all the callousness of a Renaissance prince, he sends the two courtiers to the death that had been planned for himself. (265)

In both passages Freud couples the killing of Rosencrantz and Guildenstern with that of Polonius, and his writing "Laertes" (also see Freud 1954, 224) is a slip of the pen. The slip replaces the father figure with the dispensable brother figure: Phillip, Julius, or John instead of the beloved, indispensable (but also hated) Jacob.[7] (It is perhaps significant that Freud does not make the slip in the passage addressed to the general public but in a private letter to his beloved, indispensable—but also hated—"analyst," Fliess.)

Polonius is paradoxically important in the play as the unimport-

---

speech, which employs a prime symbol for cannibalistic impatience: the rat (see Shengold 1967, 1989):

Ham. [Drawing.] How now! A rat? Dead, for a ducat, dead!
(Kills Polonius through the arras). (III.i.23)

There is also an anal-sadistic reduction here: "rat"; "ducat"—the father reduced to shit:

Ham. . . . I'll lug the guts into the neighbor room . . . (Exeunt severally, Hamlet tugging [out] Polonius). [III.i.212].

7. James Joyce in Ulysses, that novel of fathers and sons in which the hero searches for and finds a maternal father (as Mann characterizes Jacob), also shifts the focus of hatred from the father to the mother and the brothers. Joyce's theory about Hamlet, stated by Stephen Daedalus in the Scylla and Charybdis episode of Ulysses, is that the play represents Shakespeare's reaction to having been cuckolded by his brothers Edmund and Richard. Joyce thinks that Shakespeare portrays himself in the play as both old Hamlet, the murdered father, and young Hamlet, the dispossessed son (this parallels Joyce's portrayal of himself as both Bloom and Stephen in his novel). Joyce also states that Shakespeare wrote Hamlet immediately after his own father's death. This may not be true, but it corresponds with the timing of Freud's writing about Hamlet after his father's death. Joyce (who in part projects himself in his theory as Freud does in his and as anyone else would also do) emphasizes Hamlet as evidence of Shakespeare's obsession with the theme of the

ant father figure whom Hamlet can kill freely.[8] Claudius is dis-
patched only when Hamlet himself is already dying. Still, Polonius
stands for the murdered father and certainly could evoke him for
Freud. Freud even refrains from naming him in the above-quoted
passages. (See the material on the importance of names in chapter
5 below.)

In trying to account for the aggressive ambition which colored
his boyhood preoccupation with the military heroes Hannibal and
(Napoleon's) Marshal André Masséna,[9] Freud (1900b) says,

> [Perhaps] the development of this martial ideal is traceable
> still farther back into my childhood: to the times when, at the
> age of three, I was in a close relation, sometimes friendly but
> sometimes warlike, with a boy a year older than myself [my
> nephew John], and to the wishes which that relation must have
> stirred up in the weaker of us. (198)

Jones (1953) considers John "the most important person in Freud's
early childhood . . . next to his parents" (8). The relation between
the two boys was intense and ambivalent; Freud (1900) continues,

> Until the end of my third year we had been inseparable. We
> had loved each other and fought each other; and this childhood
> relationship, as I have already hinted, had a determining

"false, or usurping, or adulterous *brother*" (Blamires 1966, 90; my italics). For a
fascinating study of the meanings of Shakespeare (and Hamlet) to Freud, see Gay
1990.

8. Perhaps it is easier for Hamlet to kill the old man (who he believes is Claudius)
because he is hidden behind the arras. The scene is in his mother's private chamber
(symbolically her genitals)—almost always, at least in modern productions, her
bedchamber. Not having to see the father figure may make killing him easier.
(Oedipus kills his father, Laius, as a complete stranger.) Hamlet's father's spirit, who
can be viewed as a projection of Hamlet's mind or as an actual ghost, appears to
Hamlet in Gertrude's "closet" only after Polonius is killed. Later, when Claudius is
in full sight, Hamlet is unable to run him through (the killing becomes possible only
when Hamlet knows that he and his mother are already dying). In both "father"-
killing scenes Hamlet is with his mother. In her proximity, in identification with her,
and perhaps in displacement away from his wish to penetrate her, he can use his
sword to stab the father/king.

9. Masséna was one of Napoleon's generals; Freud believed (wrongly) that he
was of semitic origin. It furthered the boy's identification that Masséna was born a
hundred years to the day before Sigmund. Freud thought that Masséna was a
variant of the Jewish name Manasseh. The first Manasseh was the eldest son of the
biblical Joseph. In Jewish lore, stemming from the time of the Roman occupation

influence on all my subsequent relations with contemporaries. Since that time my nephew John has had many re-incarnations [424]. . . .

My emotional life has always insisted that I should have an intimate friend and a hated enemy. I have always been able to provide myself afresh with both, and it has not infrequently happened that the ideal situation of childhood has been so completely reproduced that friend and enemy have come together in a single individual. (483)

Freud wrote this at a time when he had not yet come to terms in his mind with the then-current revenant of John, Wilhelm Fliess. Fliess was the closest friend the adult Freud ever had. Theirs was a relationship that began with great promise, lasted for many years, and ended in quarreling and bitterness. Freud called Fliess his "only audience" during the years when he was developing his basic psychoanalytic ideas and working on his self-analysis. Fliess was a kind of analyst for Freud and, as in most important relationships in life, including the one to the analyst, was kaleidoscopically invested with transferences of all Freud's important early love-objects, including parents and siblings as well as nephew John.

As a child Freud had another important ambivalent, although perhaps more consistently hostile, relationship, with his half-brother Phillip, who was the same age as Freud's mother. In his early oedipal fantasies, Freud spared the beloved, feared, respected, and needed Jacob, focusing instead on Phillip as his competitor. When Freud was two and a half, just after his sister Anna was born, his nurse was dismissed for stealing. Freud asked Phillip where she had gone. He took at face value Phillip's joking answer, "Sie ist eingekastelt" (She has been put into a box), and Freud says this response became confused with his fantasies about his mother's being away after her pregnancies. (Once, later on, when the boy

of Palestine, it is written that the first Messiah would be a warrior, preparing the way for the spiritual Messiah-ben-David, who would rule forever. This military hero (conquistador) Messiah was expected to come from the seed of Joseph; he was called alternatively Messiah-ben-Joseph and, from Joseph's sons, Messiah-ben-Ephraim or Messiah-ben-Manasseh (Bakan 1958). Here was material for young Sigmund's fantasies of semitic military glory.

One cannot help wondering what it means that young Sigmund appears not to have been preoccupied with frankly military and unquestionably Jewish biblical heroes like the Maccabees or King David. (Freud's favorite, Hannibal, may have been semitic but was certainly not Jewish.)

was howling for his mother, Phillip had opened a cupboard [*Kasten* = cupboard in Austria, says Gay (1988)] to show that she was not hiding there, and Sigmund feared his mother had been put in a box like his nurse.) Jones (1953) says that Freud believed that "his half-brother and his mother, who were of the same age, had cooperated in producing the usurping Anna" (10). This made Phillip the hated rival, bypassing Jacob. The wish to attribute the paternal role to Phillip is at least unconsciously implicit in relation to an incident following the birth of Freud's youngest sibling and brother, when Sigmund was ten. Jacob had asked Sigmund to choose a name and had accepted the boy's suggestion that the infant be called Alexander after one of Sigmund's conqueror heroes, Alexander the Great, son of *Philip* of Macedon.

Freud's Philippic fantasies are evident in a dream from his seventh or eighth year which is only dimly interpreted in the Dream book (1900). He calls it an anxiety dream in which "I saw my beloved mother with a peculiarly peaceful, sleeping expression on her features, being carried into the room by two (or three) people with birds' beaks and laid upon the bed" (583). Freud associates to illustrations of Egyptian gods in Philippson's Bible. He does not mention brother Phillip but tells of a namesake who had also supplied sexual information—a concierge's son named Philipp who told him the vulgar word for intercourse: *vögeln,* derived from *Vogel* (bird). Freud had awakened from the dream screaming and had aroused his parents. He traces the anxiety back to "an obscure and evidently sexual craving that had found appropriate expression in the visual content of the dream" (584). The dream links incest, Phillip (not Jacob) as the rival, possible loss of the mother (like the nurse), and Egypt—here connoting, as for Mann's Joseph, the underworld, the sexual world, the land of the dead.

His younger brother Julius figured large in Freud's personal mythology. Freud was nineteen months old when the eight-month-old Julius died. He tells Fliess (Freud, 1954), "I welcomed my one-year-younger brother (who died within a few months) with ill-wishes and real infantile jealousy, and . . . his death left the germ of guilt in me" (219). The theme of self-reproach, founded not only on guilt for oedipal wishes but on the fulfilled wish to get rid of Julius, is dealt with in terms of many Joseph-meanings as well as in relation to many Josephs in another famous dream of Freud's, the "non vixit" dream.

The dream deals mainly with death wishes and reproaches for death wishes. The main contemporary object of the hostile wishes was Fliess (the current Julius as well as John for Freud). Freud writes to Fliess, "In my *non vixit* dream I find I am delighted to have survived you" (1954, 299). It is in connection with this dream that Freud writes of the series of revenants of John in whom "friend and enemy have come together in a single individual" (1900, 483). As had happened before with others and was to be repeated more than a few times in Freud's future, the close relationship with Fliess was heading for a breakup (still several years away), partly because Freud's self-analysis had decreased his dependency needs, partly because of Fliess's intolerance of dissent.

The entire "non vixit" dream is too long to be reproduced here, but "the central feature of the dream" was, Freud says, "a scene in which I annihilated [Josef Paneth] with a look" (422). Josef Paneth, younger than Freud, had been his successor at Brücke's Physiological Institute. One of the reasons Freud had left Brücke's laboratory was that he had little chance of advancement there; both the capable Sigmund Exner and the gifted, tragic Ernst Fleischl had positions superior to his. Freud reproached himself for contributing to Fleischl's death by his well-meant attempt to cure the older man's morphine addiction with cocaine. Freud had been shocked at Josef Paneth's open wish to have the seriously ill Fleischl out of the way, but was honest enough to realize that he himself had had the same wish when he was a demonstrator in Brücke's laboratory. "But, as was to be expected, the dream punished my friend [Josef P.] and not me, for the callous wish" (484). At the time of the dream, both Josef Paneth and Fleischl (who also appeared in the dream) were dead, as was the emperor Josef II, from whose monument the dream had borrowed the words *non* and *vixit*.

The dream is full of ghosts who return, and Freud had felt while dreaming that such beings were "people of that kind [who] only existed as long as one liked and could be got rid of if someone else [!] wished it" (421). Freud's death wishes gave him the lethal power of the basilisk,[10] able to kill with a look. This reversed a scene from Freud's past in which the father figure Brücke had crushed his

10. After his father's death, Freud had dreamed of a sign that read, "You are requested to close the eyes" (Freud 1954, 171). This not only refers to Oedipus's self-punishment of blindness but also expresses the destructive power of seeing: seeing the faults of his father, for example.

unpunctual assistant with an unforgettable piercing look of reproach from "his terrible blue eyes" (422).

The dream occurred during a time when Fliess was about to
undergo an operation. Freud was worried about him, and "the
dream thoughts now informed me that I feared for my friend's
life" (1900, 481). Freud recognized the hostile wishes toward Fliess
and connected them with desires to get rid of a series of revenants,
especially John and Fleischl, older-brother figures:

> I had replaced one Josef by another in the dream and found
> it impossible to suppress the similarities between the opening
> letters of the name "Fleischl" and ["Fliess"]. (486)

The dream is a demonstration of the hostility toward the father
(Brücke, Emperor Josef) being displaced onto brother figures.
Another Josef in the dream is Josef Breuer, who had been like a
father to Freud, helping him with advice and money. With their
joint work on hysteria, Breuer became more of an older brother.
As Freud began to outstrip Breuer in the sweep of his imagination,
increasing antagonism arose between the two, especially on Freud's
side (Jones 1953). Breuer wrote to Fliess, "Freud's intellect is soar-
ing at its highest. I gaze after him as a hen at a hawk" (Jones 1953,
242). There came a time when the hawk began to attack the hen;
Jones feels that Freud was chiefly at fault. This Josef, Breuer, had
become a revenant of John as the enemy, and the closeness between
the two men turned to "violent antipathy" (Jones 1953, 255) on
Freud's part during the last years of his friendship with Fliess. (It
may be that Freud attacked the more dispensable Breuer instead
of Fliess.) Freud owed Breuer money that for many years he was
unable to repay. The complicated relations between the two men
(Freud's part is not always a credit to him) is well described by Gay
(1988).

Freud also mentions his brother Julius in the "non vixit" dream
and connects him (and John) with Fliess. He associates to Brutus's
speech of self-justification in Shakespeare's *Julius Caesar:* "as he was
ambitious, I slew him" (III.ii.27–28). (This quote could also characterize Joseph's brothers' response to his dreams of ambition.)
Sigmund, at fourteen, had acted the part of Brutus, with John
playing Caesar (in Schiller's *Die Räuber*). In the dream Freud had
said, "My friend [Fliess] came to Vienna in July" (41), and in his
commentary he adds that July is named after Julius Caesar. Fliess,
whom Freud had regarded as a leader for so many years, was

actually slightly younger than Freud, about as much younger as Julius had been. Freud felt marked by the guilt of the survivor in relation to Julius because the infant not only had been the subject of death wishes but had actually died (see Schur 1972).

The Fliess family had asked Freud not to mention Fliess's illness to anyone. The implication that his discretion was not taken for granted offended him:

I was very disagreeably affected by the veiled reproach be- cause it was—not wholly without justification. . . . [At an earlier time] I caused trouble between two friends . . . by quite unnec- essarily telling one of them, in the course of conversation, what the other had said about him. At that time, too, reproaches had been levelled at me, and they were still in my memory. One of the two friends concerned was Professor Fleischl; I may describe the other by his first name of "Josef" [Breuer]—which was also that of P. [Josef Paneth], my friend and opponent in the dream. (1900b, 481–82)

This reproach for being a telltale and betrayer of secrets fore- shadows the final quarrel between Fliess and Freud, precipitated by Freud's unauthorized discussion with an analysand of Fliess's ideas about bisexuality. It also connects Freud with the biblical Joseph, who was reproached by his brothers for being a talebearer: "And Joseph brought bad reports of them [his brothers, the sons of Bilhah and Zilpah] to their father" (Gen. 37:2).

It is in connection with the "non vixit" dream that Freud says his own ego hides behind people named Joseph. Freud shows that any figure in a dream can stand not only for the dreamer but for any of the important people in his or her life. Parents, siblings, mate, children, friends—all can be Joseph. If Fliess, in dream or in life, was a revenant, he could represent for Freud at various times Julius, John, Phillip, or Jacob. The combinations and com- plications of trying to delineate relationships and identifications with each of the above (not to mention the possible representation of mother, sister, wife, child by a male figure) show the constantly changing complexity of human identity. To *be* Joseph, then, means being many other people at the same time. It is the analyst's daily task to try for clarity amid these complications. One can see the oversimplification involved in the (nonetheless breathtaking) in- sight contained in Freud's comment to Fliess: "And I am accustoming myself to the idea of regarding every sexual act as a process in which four persons are involved" (1954, 289).

Hostility to brothers and father is also evident in Freud's "Uncle Josef" dream (1900). The hostility is disguised by being transferred (as in *Hamlet*) to the brother of his father. The dream also provided opportunity for some direct expression of ill will toward his father, who had suffered deeply from the misconduct of his ne'er-do-well brother Josef. The dream took place at a time when Freud had been recommended for appointment as professor, so again ambition is involved. Associations to the dream led to thoughts disparaging two colleagues who had not been appointed to professorship, supposedly for reasons that would not mar Freud's hopes. Freud dreamed: "My friend R. was my uncle—I had a great feeling of affection for him." And here are his associations:

> *"R. was my uncle."* What could that mean: I never had more than one uncle—Uncle Josef. [Freud adds a footnote here: "My memory . . . was narrowed at this point. Actually I have known five of my uncles, and loved and honoured one of them."] There was an unhappy story attached to him. Once—more than thirty years ago,—in his eagerness to make money, he allowed himself to be involved in a transaction of a kind that is severely punished by the law, and he was in fact punished for it. My father, whose hair turned grey from grief in a few days, used always to say that Uncle Josef was not a bad man but only a simpleton. (1900b, 137–38)

Freud goes on to show that the feeling of affection in the dream was really hypocritical: his dream had contained a slander against R. and "in order that I might not notice this, what appeared in the dream was the opposite, a feeling of affection for him" (141). The "Uncle Josef" dream expressed hatred in a competition for the lordly position (in Vienna) of professor. And is it too fanciful to speculate that here Freud is himself uncle Josef (he was an uncle to the beloved enemy, John), not only putting himself in a position to turn his father's hair gray again but also reducing the five brothers to the one Josef? Could not the missing four brothers be Emmanuel, Phillip, Alexander, and Julius, leaving Freud "standing erect" as in the biblical Joseph's first dream of ambition?

Kings and emperors symbolize the father, illustrating the power and majesty of the head of the household as seen from the cradle.

Freud (1936) tells an anecdote about Napoleon when that ruler invoked *his* original ruler:

> Napoleon, during his coronation as Emperor in Notre Dame, turned to one of his brothers—it must no doubt have been the eldest one, Joseph—and remarked: "what would *Monsieur notre Père* have said to this, if he could have been here today?" (247)

Freud wrote this in the course of describing to Romain Rolland a peculiar feeling of unreality he had when, in fulfillment of his (conflict-ridden and therefore partially infantile and forbidden) wish to travel, he climbed the Acropolis, accompanied by his brother Alexander. He described the symptom as the result of his feeling guilty for having gone further (and seen more!) than his father. Implicit is the conquest of the mother, symbolized by climbing the hill and *looking* out at the sea. Freud was resurrecting, and faltering at reversing the consequence of, the issues touched on in the unforgettable, humiliating scene in the parental bedroom from his boyhood: this traveler, this climber of the Acropolis had something to show his father. Similarly, Joseph's climbing to the pinnacle of power in Egypt meant the fulfillment of the forbidden wish of ruling over his father and family: he was able to take care of them, showing *his* father Jacob how far his son had come.

Wittels (1924) speaks of the significance the name Joseph had for Freud and stresses the effect of the Freud family's many years of residence in the Kaiser Josef Strasse when Sigmund was growing up. Nineteenth-century writers tended to regard Emperor Josef II (1741–90) of the Holy Roman Empire as a kind of philosopher-king, contrasting his attempt to fulfill the Enlightenment ideals of liberty and equality by benevolent despotism with the repressive regime of subsequent Hapsburg kaisers. This attitude was expressed by Austria's greatest poet, Grillparzer, who in his poems would periodically trot out Josef II to give paternally reproachful lectures to his successors (Barea 1966). Josef II had abolished serfdom, curtailed the feudal privileges of the nobles, clashed openly and rudely with the pope, built many hospitals, preparing Vienna for her role as a center of medical education, and, significantly for Freud, published an Edict of Toleration for Protestants and Jews.

Freud mentions Emperor Josef II in the "non vixit" dream. And he more than once expresses the grandiose wish to supplement psychoanalysis with what he characterizes as the therapeutic power of Emperor Josef—"the benevolent interference of a powerful personage before whose will people bow and difficulties vanish"—in order to fight neurosis by alleviating the misery imposed by the realities of poverty and oppression (1916/17, 431; 1919, 167). Freud would be another powerful Joseph who could change the reality and fate of those he cared for.

The childhood wish to be emperor appears in an anecdote told by Jones (1953). Once, when Freud (having attained the rank of Professor Extraordinarius) was giving a lecture at the university,

> Abraham, Ferenczi, Rank, Sachs, and myself [Jones] were seated in the front row, he made a graceful little bow, waved his hand towards us, and murmured [as Napoleon had in the theater at Erfurt]: "*Un parterre de rois*" [a front row of kings]. (342) (Also see Grotjahn 1967, 15.)

To young Sigmund, who delighted in military heroes of semitic origin, it must have been particularly important that Josef II had granted not only equal civil rights to the Jews but also equal duties; he was the first monarch in Europe to make Jews liable for service in the army (Palmer and Colton 1965). Freud (1900b) writes,

> I can still remember sticking labels on the flat backs of my wooden soldiers with the names of Napoleon's marshals written on them. And at that time my declared favorite was already Masséna (or, to give it its Jewish form, Manasseh). (197)

The wish here was to be Manasseh, son of the powerful vizier of Egypt, and perhaps even to be the son of an emperor. Freud had bitterly contrasted his father, who had allowed a Christian to force him into the gutter and knock his hat off, with "Hamilcar Barca, [who] made his boy swear . . . to take vengeance on the Romans" (1900, 197). To be the emperor (Napoleon or Josef II) himself would mean that no antisemite would dare to force *his* father into the gutter again. He too could be Joseph, savior of Jacob. Napoleon was the son (not the oldest) who became the savior of his entire family—lifting them all up to partake of his power.

Mann makes obvious what is implicit in the Bible: that for all his hostility, the young Joseph loves his brothers. He is easily able to suppress his hatred because he has had the experience of successful narcissism. He assumes the superiority conferred both by his great natural gifts of intelligence and beauty and by the favoritism of his parents. But when his preeminence is threatened, his hatred shows.

He wants his brothers out of the way if there is any hint that one of them might obtain the blessing of the parent/god. His hatred is evident in his telling his brothers his dreams and especially in his telling them about Jacob's gift to him of the coat of many colors. It is evident in his talebearing, a fault allied to his curiosity. The defensive nature of Joseph's assertions of supremacy is obvious: the smaller brother must suppress the murderous hostility that pits him against the frightening superior strength of the older brothers. Freud says of Napoleon,

> His eldest brother was called Joseph . . . the elder brother is the natural rival; the younger one feels for him an elemental, unfathomable deep hostility for which in later life the expressions "death wish" and "murderous intent" may be found appropriate. To eliminate Joseph, to become Joseph himself, must have been Napoleon's strongest emotion as a young child. It is strange no doubt and yet it has been correctly observed that just these excessive, infantile impulses tend to turn into their opposites—the hated rival becomes the loved one. This was the case with Napoleon. We assume that he started out with an ardent hatred of Joseph, but we learn later on he loved him more than any other human being and could hardly find a fault with this worthless, unreliable man. Thus the original hatred had been overcompensated, but the early aggression released was only waiting to be transferred to other objects. Hundreds of thousands of unknown individuals had to atone for the fact that the little tyrant had spared his first enemy. (1960, 432)

Freud reversed this sequence in his relationship with Fliess (the reversal was his more characteristic pattern). The excessive admiration and love for Fliess, the man he looked up to as a kind of Messiah in their early correspondence, before the publication of *The Interpretation of Dreams,* is finally broken with, at least on the surface. Freud dismissed Fliess in a letter of 1906 as "a brutal personality."

It is also common enough for hatred for the usurping younger brother to be suppressed and reversed. Benjamin had taken Joseph's place as *the* son of Rachel, and worse, his birth had caused her death. Yet Joseph truly loved Benjamin, as Freud was apparently truly fond of Alexander. Freud's hatred for Julius was especially pathogenic because Julius had died at a time when no working over or reversal of the original impulses was possible. But siblings are relatively dispensable; hatred of the vitally needed parents is much more frightening. In his explanation of Napoleon's career of conquest and slaughter, Freud, the discoverer of what he for so long called the "father complex," strangely leaves out of the account the great man's hatred of his father, who lived until Napoleon was sixteen.

A child's primal hatred must first of all be directed outward to the mother (or the mothering figure)[11], who is at the same time gradually being distinguished from the self. The caretaking mother earns hostility as what Anna Freud (1965) calls "the first external legislator" (168). Hostility is displaced from the mother onto others—the father and siblings. The father is early on regarded as "a symbol of power, protectiveness, ownership of the mother" (186). Sexual differentiation of the people around the child becomes more important during the phallic phase of libido development, and the "oedipus complex itself . . . is based on the recognition of sex difference" (187). It is during the phallic phase, under the impact of the castration complex, that the boy most fully and frighteningly feels hostility for the father. His power to protect and his presence as a focus for masculine identification make him appear indispensable to the young boy.

The son, like Joseph or Sigmund, turns this access of oedipal hatred toward the unwelcome brothers, whom he already resents as rivals for the parent's care and love. The stories of Cain and Abel (with God's preference for Abel) and of Joseph show that hostility to the sibling exists chiefly in relation to the parent. A parent with small children can observe daily that the previously peaceful siblings often begin to quarrel *after* the parents enter the scene.

A man involved professionally in treating psychologically disturbed patients had a brother who was several years his senior (as was his analyst, whose age he had looked up in a medical directory). At the beginning, the hostility expressed in the analysis was that of a sibling rival for the love of a parent; this parent was Fortune or Fate, as with Oedipus.[12] God had smiled on the analyst, who must have been lucky enough to have the right contacts and who earned

11. Anna Freud (1965) says that infants at the beginning of life choose their objects on the basis of function, not gender.

12. It is Oedipus's last heroic, ironically pathetic attempt at denial that as he is

more, lived better, and was happy. The hatred was intense and genuinely rooted in his relationship to his brother. His parents had always played one child off against the other, training them, as it were, to become Cain and Abel. This level of hatred was rather easily voiced. In contrast, appearing later in the analysis was a terrifying and paralyzing hatred for the analyst as parent: the preoedipal "bad" mother merging into the oedipal father. In dealing with the analyst as father, fear of castration brought out the full terror of the fury that the patient expressed in life with relative freedom in his rather successful competition with brother figures. He felt free to beat out a brother, but in any competition with a father he had to lose.

For Freud, it was terrible to want to get rid of John. But at least John could fight back. It is mainly the power of the older brother that makes hating him dangerous, evoking fear of retaliation and punishment. (He is less needed than the even more powerful father, although of course in any individual instance the need can be transferred onto the older brother.) To want to get rid of Julius was worse; it is the vulnerability of the younger brother, the fear of one's own aggression, that makes hating him so dangerous. To want to get rid of Jacob combines the fear of the power of one's own murderous feelings and the fear of punitive (talion) retaliation in relation to a precious, much-needed other. Murdering the parent is then unthinkable, but it is Man's fate to think of it. Murder is part of our instinctual nature, and any access of the murderous urge is terrifying to the child. It is a lifelong burden to the human being to be in the terrible position (universally present but varying in intensity and scope for each individual) of wanting to murder those whom one feels one cannot live without. Simply feeling the murderous urges and the terrible rage that goes with them can be too much for the adult and is overwhelming to the child who has not yet developed the necessary defenses against accesses of aggression. Freud always emphasized (in his concept of inborn primal fantasies) the phylogenetic impact of the phallic phase and of the castration complex (and, it is implicit, of the preoedipal developmental phenomena that lead to these). Clinically it has seemed to me that, whatever the explanation, the intensity of hostile feeling

---

about to be crushed by Fortune, he claims Fortune as a loving parent. Why should he care who his parents are, he says, when "I am Fortune's child, not man's; her mother face hath ever smiled above me" (Sophocles).

for the parent[13] is more than can be accounted for by ontogenetic experience. The necessary search for substitutes to hate instead of the father begins with the rival brothers. This is the essence of the Joseph story for Freud.

13. The concept of the primal parent who evolves from the mother and is subsequently (for both sexes but with differences) displaced onto the father is the basic one. The Oedipus complex, which features the differentiated father and mother (who reverse roles for both sexes in the negative Oedipus complex), also contains preoedipal underpinnings related to the undifferentiated parent. The child is thus involved in conflict with and over (and in danger of losing self and/or other in relation to) two indispensable figures (in a triangle) and, more regressively and dangerously, one (in a dyad): the primal parent, the only other.

5

BIBLICAL HEROES II:

MOSES AND FREUD

In his mid-seventies, Freud again became involved with Bible stories, perhaps partly as a reaction to the Nazi persecution of the Jews. In 1934 he began to write his last completed book—on Moses. Moses, like Joseph, had long been an engrossing mythopoeic figure for Freud, appearing often in his writings (1900a, 1914b, 1939), now as a "formidable father-image" (Jones 1957), now as Freud himself. Moses, like Joseph, was associated with Egypt and had a messianic role in relation to the Jewish people, a covenant with God. His story involves some discord with his brother, Aaron, but it does not have the murderous intensity of Joseph's conflict with his brothers.[1]

Projecting the past into the future is a compulsive part of our burden as human beings that we psychoanalysts observe in ourselves and our patients; it follows that only being conscious of that past can lighten that burden. Shelley Orgel finds in Freud's *Moses and Monotheism* a message for the future of psychoanalysis from the past:

> In *Moses and Monotheism*, the great imaginative work of his last years, Freud, the dying patriarch identifying for the last time with Moses, writes about and *for* those who will follow him and keep his ideas alive after his death. He writes, as a warning and prophecy, about the killing and incorporation of the primal father, about a latency period during which the ideas of the father, equated by Freud here with God and Moses, lie dormant and in repression but are gathering strength, and about the

1. Freud certainly downplays the fraternal rivalry. Aaron appears only once in *Moses and Monotheism*. Freud even casts doubt on the fraternal relationship by describing him as "Aaron, *called* [Moses'] brother" (my italics). This is puzzling.

subsequent establishment of the father's injunctions and prohibitions (what the sons must do and what they must not do) in
the superegos of individuals and group. After an interval the
original leader's ideas are revived, and he himself may be resur-
rected years after as a mythic figure of history possessing sacred
qualities. (1990, 6–7)

Orgel focuses on the relevance of our ancestral figures for understanding what goes into the formation of our collective and individual consciences and identities. In psychoanalysis, Freud *is* our
Moses, our greatest hero; he is also our Abraham, our first leader.
Freud's preconscious awareness of this may have created difficulties
for him in relation to Karl Abraham, whose abilities as well as his
name made him both a rival and a possible successor.[2]

Freud is one of those great minds who is extremely aware of the
impact on the individual of cultural and intellectual history and
tradition. And (as I have indicated) he dealt with parental figures
in displacement onto other great minds from the past with more
comfort and less inhibition—with more conscious control, that is—
than he did directly with the current authorities in his life. Many
men and women seek out substitute parents from history and fable.
These superior beings enhance narcissistic promise, contribute,
that is, to the lure of being and having everything. Moses and
Abraham were two of a number of historical and mythical characters—actual and spiritual conquistadores—whom Freud fashioned
for his use by evolving mental images of them, changing their
identity according to his needs. These great ones from the past
provided psychic imprints of aspects of Freud's self and of his
beloved and hated others.

Freud frequently needed in fantasy to kill off his rivals and
forebears. To bring this intense wish to murder, which Freud was
to call the aggressive drive derived from the "death instinct," to
people who were *also* needed and beloved (as well as to himself)
was much more easily done in relation to relatively dispensable men
from the past, who were, after all, already dead—they were real
ghosts who could easily be made to vanish (as in the "non vixit"
dream). Focusing the drives to love and to kill on one essential
person (self or other) without whom one feels one cannot live is,

2. There were specific troubles about the priority of linking Moses with monotheism, which Karl Abraham had done long before Freud—see chapter 6 below.

as I have stated, an early psychic danger—an emotional trap that continues to exert great force throughout our developmental life. It is always more comfortable and safe to experience the conflict between accepting one's heritage and one's rage and rebellion against it at some optimal physical and temporal distance—essentially an emotional distance from primal objects, primal needs, and primal emotions (cravings and rages). To express this somewhat differently, for the safe discharge of these archaic emotions the individual requires foreigners, barbarians, as enemies. In this sense, the Egyptians and the Hebrews need each other, today as in biblical times.

Murderous rage is at the heart of Freud's interpretation of the Moses of Michelangelo (1914) and it is connected with the biblical Moses as well as with Freud's Egyptian aristocrat Moses in *Moses and Monotheism* (1939).[3]

Freud was obsessed with Michelangelo's great statue:

> For no piece of statuary has ever made a stronger impression on me than this. How often have I mounted the steep steps from the unlovely Corso di Cavour to the lonely piazza where the deserted church stands, and have essayed to support the angry scorn of the hero's glance! Sometimes I have crept cautiously out of the half-gloom of the interior as though I myself belonged to a mob upon whom his eye is turned—the mob which can hold no convictions, which has neither faith nor patience, and which rejoices when it has regained the illusory idols. (Freud 1914a, 213)

Freud was not only fearful as object of the Jehovah-like wrath of Moses toward a sinner and rebel, he was also afraid of feeling Moses' murderous wrath toward others. (He had by 1914 been subject to rebellions by Adler, Stekel, and—especially painful—by his chosen heir as head of the psychoanalytic movement, Jung.) Every individual fears both being killed and killing—in differing measure. Simply experiencing intense murderous fury is in itself terrifying to a child, underlying the associated fears of hurting and being hurt, and of losing needed others.[4] As Blum (1991) points

---

3. I refer the interested reader to the fine paper on Freud as Moses as well as on Freud in relation to Moses by Harold Blum (1991).

4. The terror of feeling murderous impulses per se perhaps coincides with Freud's automatic or traumatic anxiety, which he linked to the psychic danger of

out, Freud had a strong need to dilute, to sublimate his wrath against parents, siblings, and offspring. It is a sublimation of murder.

Moses in the biblical narrative is quickly identified as a murderer. He is first presented in Exodus as the passive object of birth, abandonment, rescue by Pharaoh's daughter, delivery to his own mother to be nursed, and so forth. Moses' first-mentioned active response is that of murder:

> One day, when Moses had grown up, he went out to his people and looked on their burdens; and he saw an Egyptian beating a Hebrew, one of his people. He looked this way and that, and seeing no one he killed the Egyptian and hid him in the sand. (57; Exod. 3:11–12)

Moses, quick to fury like Oedipus, has (also like Oedipus) a hidden and guilty secret—he not only wants to kill, he *has* killed. There is also a mass murder associated with the wrathful breaking of the first set of the tablets of the Ten Commandments (recall that Freud denies the biblical account of the breaking in *his* [1914] interpretation of *Moses*). In the Torah, after Moses has dashed the tablets to the ground in his anger at the worship of the golden calf, he gathers the sons of Levi (*his own tribe*) together:

> And [Moses] said to them, "Thus says the LORD God of Israel, 'Put every man his sword on his side . . . and slay every man his brother, and every man his companion, and every man his neighbor.'" And the sons of Levi did according to the word of Moses; and there fell of the people that day about three thousand men. (Exod. 32:27–28)

(Moses and the Lord, not content with slaughtering innocent Egyptian babies, also go in for the mass murder of rebellious Jews. Jehovah is a God of Wrath.)

Freud first saw Michelangelo's statue of Moses in 1901 and responded to it with a "flash of intuition" (Jones 1955, 20). In 1912, Freud again went to Rome and wrote his wife that he was "visiting Moses daily and might write a few words about him." This grew into a paper, published anonymously at first, "The Moses of Michelangelo" (1914a). Jones says,

---

ego dissolution (1926a). Adults react to it as an intense primal psychic danger situation. I have found this observation most helpful in understanding patients.

This essay is of special interest to students of Freud's person-ality. The fact alone that this statue moved him more deeply than any other of the many works of art with which he was familiar gives his essay on it a peculiar significance. (1955, 407)

There was certainly an identification with Moses as Freud interpre-ted him. According to Freud's interpretation of the biblical scene depicted by the Michelangelo statue, Moses (the murderer, who Freud in the 1939 book believes is also to be murdered) needs for the welfare of his people and the continuance of his work to stay his wrath and preserve the word of the Lord. Freud felt that Michelangelo had carved out "a study of character" (221)—of ad-mirable character that Freud aspired to:

for the Moses we have reconstructed will neither leap up nor cast the Tables from him. What we see before us is not the inception of a violent action but the remains of a movement that has already taken place. In his first transport of fury, Moses desired to act, to spring up and take vengeance and forget the Tables; but he has overcome the temptation, and he will now remain seated and still, in his frozen wrath and in his pain mingled with contempt. Nor will he throw away the Tables so that they will break on the stones, for it is on their especial account that he has controlled his anger; it was to preserve them that he kept his passion in check. (1914, 229–30)

Freud tells us, "This is not the Moses of the Bible . . . [but] a new Moses of the artist's conception" (230),

. . . one superior to the historical or traditional Moses. . . . [The sculptor] has added something new and more than human to the figure of Moses; so that the giant frame with its tremen-dous physical power becomes only a concrete expression of the highest mental achievement that is possible in a man, that of struggling successfully against an inward passion for the sake of a cause to which he has devoted himself. (233)

Here Freud depicts Moses as his ego ideal (see Spruiell 1985).

Freud did not want to publish his essay. He finally did so in 1914 but withheld his name from it; he did not acknowledge it as his until 1924. The reasons he gives (in a letter to Karl Abraham) seem inadequate. He calls the anonymity "a pleasantry," says he is ashamed of the essay's amateurishness and that his doubts "about the findings are stronger than usual" (Freud and Abraham 1965, 171). Jones says that a neurotic inhibition was involved, that some of Freud's doubts about his conclusions were based on the strain over the quarreling that was going on in 1913 and 1914 with and about Jung. Freud was apprehensive, in relation to *his* followers, "about whether he would now succeed in self-mastery as Michelangelo's Moses did" (1955, 367). The quarrel with Jung, Freud's chosen successor (Freud earlier compared himself with Moses, who, unlike his disciple, Joshua [Jung], would never see the promised land), involved a father/son confrontation. It also brought out hostility toward a younger man like Freud's earliest "successor," his brother Julius.[5]

In *Moses and Monotheism* Freud also interprets the breaking of the tablets of the law as symbolic of the murder of Moses by his followers; he sees this as an evocation of his postulated primal crime of the sons against the father (from *Totem and Taboo*).

To achieve any kind of higher purpose in life, fury—most specifically parricide, fratricide, and filicide—must be contained. All humans, even psychoanalysts, as Orgel indicates, even Freud (a self-characterized good hater, like Oedipus), find this very hard to do. Primal murderous fury derived from the body and the drives and also from the early inevitable frustrations of reality as mediated by the all-important parents (that is, from phylogeny and ontogeny) seems to me to be the archaic affective content of our animal natures.

I view archaic murderous rage, blending with and becoming partially neutralized by the sexual drives, as continuing to threaten our very existence and the existence of those primal objects (body

5. Freud comments on the fact that Michelangelo's statue was originally designed for the tomb of the great Pope Julius II. Julius II was a strong-willed man who could and did use violence to further his ends. Michelangelo, Freud says, "felt the same violent force of will in himself. . . . And so he carved his Moses on the Pope's tomb, not without a reproach against the dead pontiff, as a warning to himself, thus in self-criticism rising superior to his own nature" (1914a, 230). For Freud, Julius II—Il Papa—would have connoted not only brother Julius but father Jacob. This is corroborated by Freud's uninterpreted dream (inserted into the Dream book in 1914, the year the paper on Michelangelo's *Moses* was published). As a reaction to hearing church bells which woke him early on a Sunday in the Tyrol, he dreamed, "The Pope is dead" (1900b, 232). Spruiell says of *The Moses of Michelangelo*, "Once more [Freud] had been doing and undoing the murder of little Julius—a magical infantile fratricide which fronted for fantasies of two others, the crimes of patricide and filicide" (1985, 490).

parts and parents) without whom we at first feel we cannot survive (and, it follows, the existence of those people, things, and causes—as exemplified by the Tables of the Law—that take the place of those objects and supply value to our current life). Murder and cannibalism furnish a biological/instinctual bedrock to our natures; on this basis conflicts arise which can be followed, despite even optimal dilutions with maturation and transformations, in the series of psychic danger situations that evolve as the mind develops (Freud 1926a).

Both preoedipal and oedipal developmental periods feature murderous fury. This starts with cannibalism. (So many of the laws and prohibitions in the Books of Moses that constitute the Torah are about the control of cannibalism and murder.) I have found that when I ask analytic students to define the Oedipus complex, they most often leave parricide out of the oedipal combination of murder and incest. Once one is past the prime of life, with aging and approach to death, wishes to kill actual or spiritual children threaten to take preponderance over the concomitant preexisting wishes to kill parents. (Sophocles' Oedipus plays show this transition.) Seen as part of an evolving perspective, no sharply differentiated division exists between preoedipal and oedipal development. There is rather a continuum marked by transformations (Abrams' term) and regressions and progressions in which nothing ever really disappears. In the psyche, there is no once-and-for-all passing of the Oedipus complex, of the preoedipal, or of anything else, for that matter. In optimal development, despite much taming and sublimation, the murder first expressed in our cannibalistic drives continues to motivate us all.

Orgel speaks of "our continuing infantile need for great men and women in order to help curb our own drives, including patricidal and infanticidal ones" (1990, 11). We need to become aware of our human murderous heritage, of what it does to body and mind, impulses and conscience. Freud would want us to be familiar with the dynamic contrary tendencies of being enslaved to his words and wishes (as we have interpreted them) and trying to keep killing him off by breaking with his teachings. There is great resistance to the awareness of the impulses to infanticide and parricide. Knowledge of our past can help us keep to the middle ground—away from the malignant potential. But we remain psychologically burdened with the wish to murder.

I have wandered away from Freud's life. By 1934, when he was beginning to work on *Moses and Monotheism,* Freud had come a "long way from the child who devoured Thiers' story of Napoleon's power and who identified himself with the Marshal Masséna" (Bernfeld 1946, 163). Joseph was seventeen when, after expressing his overweening ambition to his brothers, he was cast into the pit to begin his struggle for greatness. Greatness came only after his separation from his father, Jacob. His dreams of glory and worship were fulfilled in Egypt. He achieved conquest (in contrast to Moses) not by killing, but by charm and especially wisdom, specifically his ability to interpret dreams. Seventeen marked an important turning point for Freud too. Adolescence meant a reawakening of hostility to his father and a renewed need to turn the oedipal wishes away from the parents onto contemporaries—brothers; but here too naked aggression is sublimated. Both Bernfeld and Jones set Freud's renunciation of military and political ambition at seventeen. "Shortly after his graduation from high school, Freud suddenly retreats from his search for power over men" (Bernfeld 1949, 169). Freud, like Joseph, "perceived that the ultimate secret of power was not force but understanding" (Jones 1953, 169).

Freud began his self-analysis when he was in his forties, and only after he had lost his father. The analysis was accomplished largely through Freud's Joseph-like ability to interpret dreams. Exploration of his own past led to mastery, to the attempt at conquest of that "unexplored region of the mind in which I have been the first mortal to set forth" (1954, 318). Freud emerges as the successful conquistador, able to disturb the peace of the world, not by blood and killing, but by understanding. It was his discovery of the Oedipus complex and his acknowledgment of his own murderous and incestuous wishes that made it possible for Freud to come to terms with Jacob and with his brothers—by changing his psychic registry of identifications and object relationships. There were inhibitions and regressions, but by and large Freud was able to transmute fratricide and parricide to psychic analysis; incest and the sexual probing of his mother's body to exploration of the human mind.

In chapter 4, I remarked on the Egyptian setting of Freud's dream about his mother. Egypt had always fascinated Freud, as it had Napoleon, of whose Egyptian campaign Freud wrote, "Where else could one go but Egypt if one were Joseph and wanted to loom large in the brothers' eyes?" (Freud 1960, 433). Freud loved to collect antiquities; his consulting room was filled with Egyptian and Greek statuettes. This collection was "his only extravagance" (Jones 1957, 297). Freud, like Oedipus, was the solver of the riddle of the Sphinx, that fabulous monster of Egyptian origin. During his last five years, the heroic, cancer-ridden man had Egypt in the background of his still active and creative mind—Egypt as a kind of ground bass against which the themes of Joseph and Moses could play in counterpoint. Freud was writing and revising his Moses book in the years from 1934 through half of 1939. Moses, according to Freud's idea, was—like Joseph, like Freud himself—a Jew, yet not a Jew. Freud felt he was an Egyptian as Joseph had become an Egyptian. In the Family Romance fantasy, the child tries to evade his impulses toward his parents by claiming another, usually a royal or divine, parentage. Moses was "found" by Pharaoh's daughter. Thus (if Freud sees himself as Moses), Pharaoh, and not the Jewish father Jacob, is the father to be reckoned with. The ambivalence inherent in the father/son confrontation figures in the Hebrew myths as the struggle between Egyptians and Jews. When Freud's book appeared in 1939, many Jews resented it because it attributed to an Egyptian the lineage and ideas of the greatest of Jewish cultural heroes (see the convincing contrary views of Yerushalmi [1991]). Moses, the godlike father figure, was presented as an Egyptian nobleman and the spiritual son of the pharaoh Ikhnaton![6]

Egypt, depicted both in the Bible and in Mann's novels as the place of refuge and plenty, of exile and persecution, had a tragic relevancy during these years as Hitler triumphed in Germany and took over Austria. The Nazi invasion of Austria finally forced the old conquistador, who in his life and in the imagery of his books so often indulged his passion for traveling, to take his penultimate great journey, to England. We know from his letters that he was thinking of earlier flights west[7]—from Israel into Egypt. His forebears also had been forced to flee west, from Palestine to Bessarabia to Cologne to Bohemia; and when he was two, his father, Jacob, had chosen, in reaction to outbreaks of antisemitism, to leave Sigmund's birthplace, Freiburg, for Leipzig and finally, Vienna.

6. Like Joseph, Freud had even had an Abraham who preceded him to Egypt; his disciple Karl Abraham had written about Ikhnaton in 1912. See chapter 6 below.

7. According to Altman (1959), *west* symbolizes death; so, according to Freud, does a *journey*.

Now the escape to England could be seen both as a journey into and a journey out of Egypt.

Egypt had been a haven offering sustenance—for Joseph fleeing from his persecuting brothers, for Jacob and his sons fleeing from famine. Up to the time of Moses, Egypt is represented in the Bible as a place for the Jews to go and live in freedom, thanks to Joseph and his providing for them the land of Goshen. But Egypt was also a land of exile and became a land of persecution. Moses led his people out of Egyptian bondage toward the promised land of Canaan. And when he did so, the Bible says,

> Moses took with him the bones of Joseph who had exacted an oath from the children of Israel, that they would take his body back to the land of Jacob. (Exod. 13:19)

For Freud, England had long been a promised land,[8] but it was also a land of exile away from the city of Vienna, loved and yet so often described in his letters to Fliess as detested and detestable,[9] but now become a beloved prison. His feelings were most ambivalent. For all his threats of leaving and mutterings of hatred for Vienna, he finally had to be forced by his children, friends, and pupils to leave the city, even after the takeover by the Nazis had

8. Freud wrote from Vienna to his fiancée, Martha, in August 1882, several months after their engagement, "I am aching for independence, so as to follow my own wishes. The thought of England surges up before me, with its sober industriousness, its generous devotion to the public weal, the stubbornness and sensitive feeling for justice of its inhabitants, the running fire of general interest that can strike sparks in the newspapers; all the ineffaceable impressions of my journey of seven years ago, one that had a decisive influence on my whole life, have been awakened in their full vividness. I am taking up again the history of the island, the works of the men who were my real teachers—all of them English or Scotch; and I am recalling what is for me the most interesting historical period, the reign of the Puritans and Oliver Cromwell with its lofty monument of that time—*Paradise Lost*, where only recently when I did not feel sure of your love, I found consolation and comfort. Must we stay here, Martha? If we possibly can, let us seek a home where human worth is more respected. A grave in the Centralfriedhof is the most distressing idea I can imagine." Jones adds, "And in the end his bones did not repose, after all, in that dreaded Viennese cemetery, but in his beloved England" (Jones 1953, 178–79). Cromwell and Milton should be added to the list of Freud's ego ideal figures.

9. Freud (from a letter to Fliess of March 11, 1900): "I hate Vienna with a positively personal hatred, and, just the contrary of the giant Antaeus I draw fresh strength whenever I remove my feet from the soil of the city which is my home" (1954, 311).

made the hatred unmistakably justifiable. Not only was he leaving behind the many, many years of his past, he was also separating himself from the bones of his parents. The grave evokes the womb. For Joseph, this meant the cave of Machpelah, where he could lie at peace with his ancestors. But Joseph was never buried with either Rachel or Jacob. His tomb lies apart, as does Freud's, as does that of Oedipus, who was not permitted burial in Athens ("the city, our mother") but only at nearby Colonus. The city symbolizes the mother, and to come to final terms with that first object of hostility and love is to return to earth in a hallowed spot. It was perhaps in these regressive, chthonic, and eschatological senses that Freud longed for Vienna.

Freud was very ill, very much aware of his old age and of his identity as father and patriarch. He was no longer Joseph going down to Egypt to triumph over his brothers. He was now identified with a greater and older rival, Jacob. The biblical Jacob had gone to Egypt to be reunited with his lost son, Joseph, and was to die there in exile. It is as Jacob that Freud, awaiting emigration in Vienna, writes to his son Ernst in England:

> Two prospects keep me going in these grim times: to rejoin you all and—to die in freedom [last four words in English]. I sometimes compare myself with the old Jacob who, when a very old man, was taken by his children to Egypt, as Thomas Mann is to describe in his next novel. Let us hope it won't be also followed by an exodus from Egypt. It is high time that Ahasuerus[10] came to rest somewhere. (Freud 1960, 442)

The role of Jacob here condenses Freud as father, his own father, the biblical patriarch, and the Wandering Jew. Freud was going to England to die:

> To go back to the earth in London
> An Important Jew who died in exile. (Auden 1939, 163)

The great road from childhood to paternity had been completely traversed, the drive for power over father and brothers for the possession of mother and sisters had been transcended. He had now become a patriarch, the undisputed leader of a new way of thinking about, understanding, and helping human beings. To repeat the quotation with which I began this book:

10. Ahasuerus: the Wandering Jew—forced, like Oedipus, to travel for his sins.

To us he is no more a person
Now but a whole climate of opinion. (Auden 1939, 167)

And just before he crossed the English Channel, the ambition of his adolescent years showed itself again. The old man dreamt of himself as William the Conqueror![11] The wish to be the conquistador—Moses entering, Messiah-ben-Joseph conquering, the promised land—still stirred as he was about to embark on the last journey.

11. Could this have been a last unconscious stirring toward Wilhelm (William) Fliess?

6

FLIESS, KARL ABRAHAM, AND FREUD

Freud's interest in Jewish heroes began in his childhood as part of his "early familiarity with the Bible story (at a time before I had learnt the act of reading . . . [which had] . . . as I recognized much later, an enduring effect upon the direction of my interests" (1925, 8). We do not know the extent of the influence on him (by way of his Catholic nanny) of the New Testament and its Jewish hero Jesus; the child Sigmund (like so many others) was not necessarily aware of the Jewishness of Christ.[1] One can assume an ambiguous confluence of Jewish and anti-Jewish feelings in Freud's nursery years that was partly linked with his nurse and her fate.

I have noted that Freud associated himself with Jewish figures from the Bible stories. Any Jewish boy (even if his father was not named Jacob) would resonate with the story of Jacob's father, Isaac, who was almost sacrificed by his father, the Jewish Ur-father, Abraham. I have cited Freud's disillusion with his father when Jacob told his son how he had allowed a gentile to knock off his fur hat and throw it into the gutter, saying, "Jew, get off the pavement!" When the boy asked what Jacob had then done, he "calmly replied, 'I stepped into the gutter and picked up my cap'" (Jones 1953, 22). This cautious behavior was not what Sigmund wanted from his father, and not what he (the future conquistador) had looked for in the Jewish father figures in the Bible. Mordecai had refused to bow down to Haman's hat. How could his father have allowed *his* hat to be defiled by a persecuting gentile without even a protest? To hear from Jacob's lips, from that father who had said that his son would come to nothing, that a Christian could get away with treating *him* as "nothing" was a great burden to the boy, who had

---

1. Blum (1991) has speculated about the impression on Freud of the statue of an Old Testament prophet that used to stand in front of the church at Freiburg and could easily have been construed as a statue of Moses.

to suppress his fury and wish for revenge toward his father. I have noted Freud's contrasting Jacob's masochistic behavior to that of Hannibal's father, Hamilcar, who "made his son . . . swear on the household altar to take vengeance on the Romans. . . . [Freud] said that ever since then Hannibal had a place in his phantasies" (Jones 1953, 22–23). Freud's identification with Hannibal, the heroic attacker of Rome, was passionate; the boy made much of the myth that the Carthaginians were descended from the Phoenicians and were therefore of semitic origin. Freud mourned Hannibal's ultimate defeat much as the prophetic Dido does at the end of Berlioz's great opera. And as a man he associated his inhibitions about visiting Rome with Hannibal's inability to get to his enemy's capital. (We know that Freud also identified himself as a Roman: with Brutus, the Julius killer.)

Biblical (and Greek and Roman) figures continued to influence Freud throughout his life in relation to those he regarded as substitute fathers, brothers, and sons (and, to a lesser extent as far as we know, mothers, sisters, and daughters). Biblical identifications and references to biblical figures are therefore especially meaningful and abundant in relation to those who were closest to Freud professionally and emotionally: Breuer, Fliess, Jung, and Abraham—the last a biblical namesake like his father, Jacob.

Karl Abraham was the ablest of Freud's followers and, if not the most beloved, probably the most successful over the years in winning and retaining Freud's respect. Very little has been written about or by Karl Abraham that does not make us admire him. His character exhibits the uprightness, courage, and candor of the hero of a romantic novel. There seems also to have been a quality of stiffness and emotional distance, which suggests (at our reader's remove) that he may have lacked some fullness of emotional and psychological dimensionality like the heroes of the novels of Walter Scott or the early George Eliot. One can picture Abraham as an intellectual Ivanhoe or a wise and sophisticated Adam Bede. Jones (1927) calls him a "preux chevalier of science, sans peur et sans reproche" [a valiant knight of science, without fear and without blame] (41). In his obituary notice of the much younger man, Freud pays tribute to Abraham's honest and pure character, applying to him Horace's "interger vitae scelerisque purus" (he whose life is blameless and free of guilt) (1926b, 277).

Perhaps so much virtue was intimidating—frequently a certain holding at a distance on Freud's part is perceptible in their letters.

This was noted by others. Wilhelm Reich wrote, "[Freud] also liked Abraham very much, but not very personally. He respected him" (1967, 68). And Jones (1955) wrote,

> [Abraham's] distinguishing attributes were steadfastness, common sense, shrewdness and a perfect self-control. However stormy or difficult the situation he retained his unshakable calm. . . . [He] appeared to have no need for any specially warm friendship. . . . One would scarcely use the word "charm" in describing him; in fact, Freud used sometimes to tell me he found him "*too Prussian.*" But Freud had the greatest respect for him. (159; my italics)

Abraham's coolness may have been useful in his repeated assumption of the thankless role of the disciple having to admonish his leader. The vicissitudes of his relationship with Freud can be followed in their published correspondence. Despite occasional disagreements and disputes, the disciple shows little envy; the leader listens, learns, respects. But Abraham did not evoke the passionate attachments Freud felt for Fliess and Jung—intensifications of his calmer adolescent feelings for his boyhood friend Eduard Silberstein.

Abraham was in the second generation of analysts. He met Freud in 1907, when he was thirty and Freud fifty-one, but he had been studying the older man's work since 1904 (Jones 1955, 38). Their friendship lasted until Abraham's death in 1925. Abraham's writings support and supplement Freud's work; they are full of original observations and ideas, insights that were absorbed by and often even inspired the older man. While Freud calls himself a good hater (in letters to the like-minded and abetting Jung he even shows himself to be a zestful one), it has been said of Abraham that although he could fight, he could not hate (Grotjahn 1968, 10). Abraham's fairness and calm made him Freud's guide and helper in many distressing factional quarrels, particularly in the course of the defections of Jung and Rank.

Abraham's great intellectual abilities are not those of a towering genius, like Freud; and he does not appear to have Freud's heroic character—heroic in the Aristotelian sense: full of conflict, defects, and quirks. Yet both men dedicated themselves to struggling to search out the truth, no matter where such inquiry might lead. This ardent moral quest is what makes Freud the greatest of psychoanalysts as well as the first. But human failings are apparent in Freud's work and in his life. (We know less about Abraham's.) Freud was generally not as good a *Menschenkenner* (judge of people) in his personal life as was Abraham (Grotjahn 1968, 10; Glover 1965, xii, xv). This sometimes put Abraham in the reversed role in relation to Freud of the child admonishing the parent. Inevitably this and other transferences and identifications influenced Freud's reactions to Abraham, and Abraham's to Freud; the strains this evoked in both men are evident in their letters. Jones wrote, "At times Abraham almost assumed the attitude of an analyst towards Freud who did not want to admit a painful truth" (1957, 54)—and the analyst draws onto himself feelings from all the important figures in the patient's life.

Freud was old enough to regard Abraham as a son. Abraham was, after the defection of Jung (who was the same age), Freud's chosen successor as the leader of the psychoanalytic movement. Abraham could also appear as a younger brother. And in his roles as adviser and arbiter, Abraham could be felt not only as a father but as an older brother: the twenty-year age difference between the men was the same as that between Sigmund and his half-brother Phillip, to whom, when Freud was four, partly because Phillip was just the age of Sigmund's mother, the boy had attributed the paternity of his unwanted younger sister, Anna. Abraham could figure unconsciously for Freud as a father because his name linked him with the biblical Father Abraham. Mother and sister could be involved for Freud too—not only in relation to rivalry *for* them, but also, by way of feminine identification, rivalry *with* them. As I will outline, passive and homosexual wishes were aroused in Freud as part of his reaction to Abraham's reliance in his last illness on Wilhelm Fliess, the man who had evoked more of the "feminine side" (Freud 1954, 302) of the adult Freud than any other man.

My interest in the relationship between Freud and Abraham was augmented by my noticing a surprising and totally uncharacteristic omission on Freud's part in his *Moses and Monotheism* (published in 1939) of a paper by Abraham, written in 1912, in which some of Freud's conclusions about Moses and monotheism are prefigured.[2] Freud was scrupulous about assigning priorities and crediting others, so there are many citings of Abraham's contributions to, and

2. After I had published a paper on the slip (Shengold 1972), I learned that it had previously been pointed out by Velikovsky in his book *Oedipus and Ahknaton* (1960).

initiation of, his ideas (for example, Freud 1911, 40, 70, 76; 1917b, 249, 250; 1925, 61; 1931, 25), especially in relation to dementia praecox, female sexuality, and melancholia. There is one significant exception to Freud's scrupulousness involving priority, although it is a transient one and took place before Freud met Abraham. Freud describes it himself:

> One day in the summer of 1901 [actually 1900] I remarked to a friend [Wilhelm Fliess] with whom I used at that time to have a lively exchange of scientific ideas: "These problems of the neuroses are only to be solved if we base ourselves wholly and completely on the assumption of the original bisexuality of the individual." To which he replied: "That's what I told you two and a half years ago at Br. [Breslau] when we went for that evening walk. But you wouldn't hear of it then." It is painful to be requested in this way to surrender one's originality. I could not recall any such conversation or this announcement of my friend's. One of us must have been mistaken and on the "*cui prodest?*" [who profits from it?] principle it must have been myself. Indeed, in the course of the next week I remembered the whole incident, which was just as my friend had tried to recall it to me; I even recollected the answer I had given him at the time: "I've not accepted that yet; I'm not inclined to go into the question." But since then I have grown more tolerant when, in reading medical literature, I come across one of the few ideas with which *my name* can be associated, and find that *my name* has not been mentioned. (1901, 143–44; my italics)

We shall see the theme of bisexuality and the person of Wilhelm Fliess reappear in relation to Freud's not mentioning Abraham's *name*.

Abraham's work of 1912 was "Amenhotep IV: A Psycho-Analytical Contribution Towards the Understanding of His Personality and of the Monotheistic Cult of Aton." By 1934, when he started to write about Moses again, Freud must have "forgotten" Abraham's paper, which he had greeted in his letters to Abraham in 1912, discussed with other colleagues, and referred to as late as 1923 (Freud and Abraham 1965, 334). It was after Abraham's death that the slip of the mind occurred; a parapraxis is a complicated mental event whose many meanings cannot be fully explored without the cooperation of the one who made it. I am going to attempt a speculative analysis in the hope of arriving at some of the complex meaning that one person can have for another. The complexity is compounded in this case by the evocative associations of Karl Abraham's name, which, I feel, connected him for Freud with his biblical namesake.

Abraham was confident of Freud's involvement in his work on Amenhotep because he knew Freud was fascinated with Egypt, as evidenced by the collection of Egyptian statues and objects he had seen in Freud's office.[3] Abraham refers to these interests of Freud's in his letter of January 11, 1912, announcing the new paper:

> I know its theme will interest you: it is about Amenhotep IV and the Aton cult. The subject has a *peculiar attraction* for me—to analyze all the manifestations of repression and substitute formation in a person who lived 3,300 years ago. The Oedipus complex, sublimation and reaction formation—all exactly as in a neurotic of the present day. I did the preparatory work in the Egyptian department of the Berlin museum and was reminded more than once *of the first introduction to Egyptology that I enjoyed in Vienna in 1907*. (Freud and Abraham 1965, 111–12; my italics)

The "peculiar attraction" of Egypt, derived from the father figure Freud, must have contributed to Abraham's motivation to write his historical essay about an Egyptian father/son conflict in which the son breaks away from the father's beliefs—especially relevant at a time when there was a struggle over the succession for leadership of the psychoanalytic movement. (Jung and Abraham, who was junior to Jung at Burghölzli sanatorium in Zurich, never liked each other.) Freud responds to Abraham's announcement with great excitement: "Just think of it, Amenhotep IV in the light of psychoanalysis. That is surely a great advance in orientation" (Freud and Abraham 1965, 112). The progress of the work is discussed in several more letters; Freud suggests including a portrait of "the interesting king" (116) and tells Abraham that

3. The Wolf Man (1971) describes Freud's office as it was in 1910: "I can remember, as though I saw them today, his two adjoining studies, with the door open between them and with their windows opening on a little courtyard. There was always a feeling of sacred peace and quiet here. The rooms themselves must have been a surprise to any patient, for they in no way reminded one of a doctor's office but rather of an archaeologist's study. Here were all kinds of statuettes and other unusual objects, which even the layman recognized as archaeological finds from ancient Egypt. Here and there on the walls were stone plaques representing various scenes of long-vanished epochs" (139).

Imago, the psychoanalytic magazine for applied analysis, was "eagerly awaiting your Amenhotep" (116). In his reply, Abraham accepts the suggestion about the portrait and adds that he will also print a picture of the sun-worshipper's mother, Queen Tiy (thereby bringing up between these two men the third figure in an oedipal triangle).

In his paper, Abraham describes Amenhotep IV as the "first great man in the realm of ideas in recorded history" (1912, 263). The young pharaoh rebelled against polytheism, especially against Amon, the chief god of his father, and put Aton, the sun god, in Amon's place. At the age of seventeen, Amenhotep changed his name (which was the same as his father's) to Ikhnaton, "he who is agreeable to Aton," and established the sun god as the *only* god. He had Amon's name effaced even from the monuments to his own father, Amenhotep III (this involved erasing his father's name). Ikhnaton, when Queen Tiy died, put his mother's body not in his father's tomb but in one meant for himself. Abraham tells an oedipal story of a son who tries to efface his father's identity and replace him, making claim to the body of his mother.

Freud could have identified with the young Egyptian when he read Abraham's paper (as he identified throughout his life with Moses, whom in his last book he calls an Egyptian). Ikhnaton was, like Freud, an intellectual who had turned away from war and conquest. Ikhnaton's renunciation had come when he was seventeen, Freud's age when, according to Jones (1953, 348), he turned away from military ideals and toward understanding the life of the mind.[4] Ikhnaton also was a writer: that he described himself as "the king who lives for the truth" would have enhanced Freud's feelings of identification. Freud's involvement is seen in a letter written after

4. The shift away from military ambition is evidenced in the recently published letters of Freud to his friend Eduard Silberstein (Freud 1990), written when he was aged sixteen to twenty-six. There is no sign of Sigmund's fierce ambition to conquer in the rather bland and timid correspondence, in which it is not military conquest but sexual conquest that Freud is conflicted about. His wishes are expressed at a shy remove here and in a Spanish setting (the letters were written in Spanish). But for Freud the wish to be the bold conquistador (a Spanish word) remained hidden. When he was twenty-nine, he wrote to his fiancée, Martha, expressing in biblical metaphor his wishes to be like Hannibal and Napoleon: "[Breuer] told me he had discovered that *hidden* beneath the surface of timidity there lay in me an extremely daring and fearless human being. I have always felt as though I had inherited all the defiance and the passions with which our ancestors defended their Temple and could sacrifice my life for one great moment in history" (1960, 202; my italics).

he received the manuscript of Abraham's paper: "I have read your Egyptian study with the pleasure that I always derive both from your way of writing and your way of thinking." Freud goes on to make two "criticisms or suggestions for alteration." He wonders about Abraham's generalization that "when the mother is particularly important the conflict with the father takes milder forms. I have no evidence of this." (One would certainly agree with Freud's objection to the generalization; he may have been thinking of his own oedipal involvement.) The other criticism, which is also well founded, reflects Freud's thinking of himself in relation to Ikhnaton. He has "doubts about representing the king so distinctly as a neurotic, which is in sharp contrast with his exceptional energy and achievements, as we associate neuroticism . . . with the idea of inhibition. *We all have these complexes,* and we must guard against calling everyone neurotic" (1965, 118–19; my italics).[5] Abraham accepts the suggestions: "I shall revise it. . . . I shall only compare Ikhnaton with the neurotic patient" (1965, 119).

Freud could have been affected by Abraham's reference to the relations between Ikhnaton and the father as symbolized by the sun. Freud had recently written about the paternal significance of the sun in his paper on the Schreber case (1911). He described Schreber's defiance of the sun by staring into it. This was referred to by Abraham in the letter to Freud that expressed his intention of putting a picture of Tiy, "the sun-worshipper's mother" (1965, 117), in his Ikhnaton paper. Abraham writes about having seen two patients who, like Schreber, could "stare into the sun without flinching. The photophobia[6] proved to be directly connected with the father . . . the paternal sun" (1965, 117). Freud had written in the 1911 work,

> And when Schreber boasts that he can look into the sun unscathed and undazzled, he has rediscovered the mythological method of expressing his filial relation to the sun, and has confirmed us once again in our view that the sun is the symbol of the father. (81–82)

What Freud calls "the delusional privilege" (1911, 81) of being

5. In 1912 Freud had not yet fully accepted that neurosis (or worse) is inherent to being human.

6. The slip for *photophilia* perhaps shows the ambivalence of the usually unflinching Abraham when he faces Freud as the father figure.

able to gaze at and defy the father-sun with open eyes is to be contrasted with Freud's attitude toward his own father as expressed after Jacob's death in 1896 in "a very pretty dream on the night after the funeral: I found myself in a shop where there was a notice up saying:

You are requested
To close the eyes." (1954, 171)

Freud calls the dream "an outlet for the feeling of self-reproach which a death generally leaves among the survivors" (171). The "request" is also a mild statement of the terrible reproach and demand for punishment by Oedipus's conscience that drove him to blind himself. Freud's preoccupation with vision and insight, his father's eyes and his own, and with light and blindness is amply documented in *The Interpretation of Dreams* and in Jones's biography (see Shengold 1966).

Abraham's paper compares Ikhnaton to Phaeton, son of the sun god, Helios, who "had the temerity to seek to drive the chariot of the sun across the heavens in the place of his father" (1912, 290) and, unable to hold the horses, fell and was killed. Abraham ends his paper with this parable, saying that Ikhnaton, like Phaeton, "in striving to reach the height of the sun . . . dropped the reins which his forefathers had held with a strong hand, and so shared the fate of many an idealist: living in their world of dream, they perish in reality" (290). This was a strong warning to the son who wants to climb higher than his father. One is reminded of Freud's reactions on climbing the hill of the Acropolis.[7]

We have seen that Freud's interest in Egypt began with his childhood involvement in the Bible. Part of the child's interest was determined by his Oedipus complex. I will repeat the eight-year-old Freud's dream which I commented on in chapter 4:

I saw my beloved mother, with a peculiarly peaceful, sleeping expression on her features, being carried into the room by two (or three) people with birds' beaks and laid upon the bed. I woke in tears and screaming, and interrupted my parents' sleep. The strangely draped and unnaturally tall figures with birds' beaks were derived from the illustrations to Phillipson's Bible. I fancy

7. According to Jones, Freud compared his "curious attack of obfuscation" (1955, 147) on the Acropolis in 1904 to his fainting attacks of 1906–12. The latter attacks involve Abraham, Jung, and Egypt: see below.

they must have been gods with falcons' heads from an ancient Egyptian funerary relief. (1900b, 583–84)

Freud associates to the German street word for sexual intercourse: *vögeln*, derived from *Vogel*, bird. He remembers waking up afraid that his mother was dying or dead and attributes the anxiety in the dream to "an obscure and evidently sexual craving" (584). The funerary relief from an illustrated Bible which provided the scenario for this dream might well have been evoked again by Abraham's writing of the burial of Queen Tiy in the tomb destined for her son:

> Tiy's embalmed body was not interred beside that of her consort, but in a new mausoleum near the city of Aton, in which Ikhnaton himself one day wished to rest. . . . His rivalry with his father for the possession of his mother was to extend beyond the grave. *So he realized with the dead what he was unable to achieve with the living.* In this respect he particularly reminds us of the behavior of neurotics. (Abraham 1912, 274; my italics)

One might add—and particularly of the *dreams* of neurotics.

Chapter 5 above has told of Freud's lifelong involvement with Moses, sometimes as an alter ego: "the man who dared to challenge God and was punished" (Kanzer 1969, 197), sometimes as "the formidable father-imago" (Jones 1955, 364). Freud writes of feeling that Michelangelo's statue of Moses was sometimes looking at him scornfully, as if he were one of the rebellious multitude. Abraham, the author of a paper on Moses, was often in his later contact with Freud in the position of feeling reluctantly obliged to reproach the older man.

In *The Interpretation of Dreams*, Freud connects Moses with another "Prussian" besides Karl Abraham, in fact an arch-Prussian: Otto von Bismarck. The reference to Moses was made in relation to a dream of the Iron Chancellor's, analyzed by Hanns Sachs and interpolated in Freud's Dream book in 1919. The dream contains a scene

> of a miraculous liberation from need by [Bismarck's] striking a rock and at the same time calling on God as a helper; [this] bears a remarkable resemblance to the biblical scene in which Moses struck water from a rock for the thirsting Children of Israel. . . . It would not be unlikely that in this time of conflict Bismarck should compare himself to Moses, the leader, when

the people he sought to free rewarded him with hatred, rebellion and ingratitude. (Freud 1900b, 380)

Freud goes on to point out the masturbatory fantasy involved both in Bismarck's dream and in the biblical story of Moses seizing the rod. (So Moses becomes the rebellious masturbator.) Bismarck, says Freud, identified himself with Moses in the dream and even went beyond Moses by being permitted to enter the promised land.

According to Jones, Freud was fascinated by Bismarck, and

Freud's father had been such an ardent admirer of Bismarck, on the grounds of German unification, that when he had to translate the date of his birthday from the Jewish calendar into the Christian one he chose that of Bismarck. [Both men had been born in 1815.] Freud once asked his friend Fliess whether his numerical computations could predict which of the two men would die first. (Jones 1953, 192)

There was then ambivalence in Freud about Bismarck stemming in part from ambivalence about his father, and death wishes were involved. In the 1880s, Freud wrote to his fiancée that "Bismarck like a nightmare [*Alp*, in German] weighed heavily on the whole continent: his death would bring universal relief" (Jones 1953, 192).

Abraham, in at least three places in his paper, links *Moses* and *monotheism* to Ikhnaton, whom he describes as a harbinger of Moses:

Ikhnaton's teachings not only contain essential elements of the Jewish *monotheism* of the Old Testament, but are in many ways in advance of it. . . . Ikhnaton does not imagine [God] as corporeal, like the old gods, but as spiritual and impersonal. He therefore forbids all pictorial representation of this god, thus making himself in this respect a forerunner of *Moses* the lawgiver. (1912, 275; my italics)

Later in the paper:

The belief in a single divine being, invisible to man, would certainly not have conquered the minds of the people. This fact . . . also explains why the *monotheism* of *Moses*, which chronologically came soon after the Aton cult, appealed so little to the people. (285; my italics. This last statement could easily lead to Freud's ideas about Michelangelo's Moses.)

Toward the end of his paper, Abraham says that Ikhnaton made Aton

> the one and only god, in transparent imitation of the uniqueness of the father. He thereby became the precursor of *Moses and his monotheism,* in which the one and only god unmistakably bears the features of the patriarch, the sole ruler of the family. (287; my italics)

Abraham himself bears the name of the first patriarch.

These allusions to Moses and monotheism must have been suppressed by Freud when he was writing his Moses book, in which he identifies Moses as a follower of Amenhotep IV. In that 1939 book Freud reviews the entire story of Amenhotep IV—his rebellion against the god of his father, the establishment of the monotheistic worship of Aton—but without mentioning the paper that had so impressed him in 1912. Freud believed that Moses was a follower of Ikhnaton and perhaps had even been in contact with him. By declaring that Moses was an Egyptian, Freud deprived the Jews of one of their culture-heroes.

Freud had forgotten that, as with Moses, an Abraham had preceded him in Egypt. Indeed, Freud's book neglects the biblical Abraham too. Freud regarded Moses as a historical figure and called the patriarchs Abraham, Isaac, and Jacob legendary inventions, introduced after the time of Moses (the name of Freud's father's namesake is thereby erased). One of the arguments Freud advances in his claim that Moses was an Egyptian has to do with his assertion that Moses introduced circumcision to the Jews. He cites Herodotus, who claims that circumcision was an Egyptian custom, and Freud concludes that it was derived from the Egyptians by the Jews. In making this argument, Freud dismissed as a later "clumsy invention" (45) the references in Genesis to circumcision as part of the covenant God made with Abraham. If one assumes the historical validity of Abraham, a consistent argument could be made that the story of Abraham dwelling in Egypt represents some historical truth; and the Egyptians might have derived the custom from the Hebrews long before Moses. Freud's view dissociated circumcision from Father Abraham and also from Jacob by depriving them of their historical existence. Moses replaces Abraham as the true father of the Jewish people.

The Egyptian-Hebrew confrontations in the Bible represented a passionate issue for Freud; he was sometimes on one side, sometimes on the other. In chapter 4 I discussed the ambivalent meaning Egypt had for Freud in relation to his lifelong identification with Joseph, son of Jacob. Harry Slochower pointed out to me that Abraham was not only the first patriarch but the first *Jew,* and that therefore Freud's guilt over denying Moses' Jewishness (and, I would add, denying Abraham's historical existence) might have led him to displace his guilt to Abraham's namesake, Karl Abraham.

The name *Abraham* would seem a superficial factor in the Freud-Abraham relationship. But (Karl Abraham says) Ikhnaton's patricidal impulse was directed against the *name* of his father. It was in part because of Abraham's paper of 1911 "On the Determining Power of Names" that Freud became aware of "the importance of names in unconscious mental activities" (1913, 56).[8] One can assume that Freud's early interest in the patriarch Abraham was part of his fascination with the Bible stories. The name itself, according to the Torah, means "father of a multitude" (26). When Yahweh grants the name Abraham to his favorite Abram he tells him, "And you shall no longer be called Abram, but your name shall be Abraham, for I make you the father of a multitude of nations" (Gen. 17:3). This is followed by the covenant about circumcision: "The covenant which you shall keep between me and you and your offspring to follow: every male among you shall be circumcised" (17:10). This was the covenant Freud describes as a later invention in *Moses and Monotheism.* Father Abraham is mentioned elsewhere in Freud's writings in relation to the sacrifice of Isaac. Perhaps the association of this primal father with circumcision and filicide conditioned some of Freud's hostile attitudes toward Karl Abraham.

As this chapter continues its meandering *fugato,* the reader may not be aware that a chronological sequence is being followed. Shortly after the publication of Abraham's Ikhnaton paper (1912), Carl Gustav Jung made his full entrance in the Egyptian drama.[9] Freud met Jung in early 1907; at the end of the year Freud had his first meeting with Abraham, with whom he had previously exchanged letters. Jung, like Abraham, had been interested in

8. Abraham wrote, confirming Stekel's observation, "The bearer of a particular name often feels he has a duty to it . . . certainly one finds that a boy who has the same . . . name as a famous man tries to emulate him, or shows an interest in him in some other way" (1911, 31). There is no evidence that I am aware of, however, that Abraham saw *himself* as the first patriarch.

9. In his autobiography, Jung (1961) tells us that, as a boy his "schoolmaster hung the nickname 'Father Abraham' on me . . . [I] could not understand why . . .

Freud's ideas for several years prior to the meeting. A regular correspondence between Freud and Jung began in 1906, and Freud felt "elation" (Jones 1955, 35) that his ideas were finding acceptance at the famous psychiatric clinic at Zurich (Burghölzli), where the great Bleuler was the professor and Jung his chief assistant. Together with the favorable impression Jung made in person, it was very hard, Jones (1955) says, for Freud to

> retain a cool judgment . . . For two or three years . . . Jung's admiration for Freud and enthusiasm for his work were unbounded. His encounter with Freud he regarded as the high point of his life, and a couple of months after the first meeting he told him that whoever had acquired a knowledge of psychoanalysis had eaten of the tree of Paradise and attained vision. Freud on his part was not only grateful for the support that had come to him from afar, but was also very attracted by Jung's personality. He soon decided that Jung was to be his successor and at times called him his "son and heir." (35, 37)

Jones paraphrases a letter from Freud to Jung of February 28, 1908, in which the older man says that "Jung was to be the Joshua destined to explore the promised land of psychiatry which Freud, like Moses, was only permitted to view from afar" (1955, 37). In 1910, Freud appointed Jung president of the International Psycho-Analytical Association, to the resentment of many of Freud's Viennese followers.

Abraham had worked at Burghölzli for three years (1904–07) under Bleuler and Jung, and this apparently gave him a less-than-favorable impression of the Swiss group and specifically of Jung. Very soon, there was a good deal of mutual hostility between the psychoanalysts from Vienna (mostly Jewish) and the Swiss (mostly gentile); Freud was obliged again and again to make peace, although his feelings seem to have been more often with the Swiss than with his fellow Viennese. Abraham, by then practicing in Berlin, was for a while outside the quarrel and was called upon by Freud to help patch things up. But at the Salzburg Congress in 1909 Jung and Abraham had clashed, personally and over scientific

---

yet somewhere in the background I felt the name had hit the mark" (66). We do not know if Freud knew about this Abraham identification of Jung's, but it is possible since, according to Jung, for some weeks in 1909 the two men met "every day and analyzed each other's dreams" (1961, 178).

matters. Freud at first did not want to recognize Jung's antagonism to major psychoanalytic assumptions. By 1912, Abraham and Freud were in disagreement about Jung, and Freud was extremely worried about his followers' differences and the future of the psychoanalytic movement. It was in this setting that the penultimate meeting between Freud and Jung occurred, and its most dramatic happening was connected with Karl Abraham's Amenhotep paper.

Five of Freud's chief followers had been called to a meeting in Munich in November of 1912 to consider the idea of founding a new analytic magazine. The matter was settled positively and quickly. Freud and Jung then took a long walk before lunch in which they discussed their differences. According to Jones,

> Freud . . . had steam to let off and did not spare him a good fatherly lecture. Jung accepted all the criticisms and promised to reform. . . . Freud was in high spirits at the luncheon, doubtless elated at winning Jung round again. There was a little discussion about Abraham's recent paper on the Egyptian Amenhotep . . . in which Abraham traced the Egyptian king's revolution to deep hostility against his father. . . . Jung protested that too much was made of Amenhotep's *erasing of his father's name* and inscriptions wherever they occurred; any such death wishes were unimportant in comparison with the great deed of establishing monotheism . . . then Freud started to criticize the Swiss for their recent publications in Zurich where his work and even *his name* were being ignored. (1955, 146–47; my italics)

Jung defended himself, and Jones had the impression that Freud was taking the matter rather personally:

> Suddenly, to our consternation, [Freud] fell on the floor in a dead faint. The sturdy Jung swiftly carried him to a couch in the lounge where he soon revived. His first words as he was coming to were strange: "How sweet it must be to die." (Jones 1953, 317)

This was Freud's third fainting fit in the same room in the Park Hotel in Munich. The earlier two had occurred in 1906 and 1908. There had also been one in 1909 in Bremen when Jung was present. On both occasions with Jung there had just been an argumentative discussion on the topic of death wishes, and on both occasions Jung had reproached [Freud] for attaching too much importance to them (Jones 1955, 147).

In his autobiography Jung describes the two fainting attacks he witnessed. In 1909 in Bremen, Jung had kept discussing "peat-bog corpses" (prehistoric men drowned or buried in the peat marshes of northern Europe, whose bodies had been preserved by the chemicals in the bog water: "a natural mummification") (Jung 1961, 156). (The allusion to mummies would certainly have unconsciously evoked Egypt here.) Jung continues,

> This interest of mine got on Freud's nerves. "Why are you so concerned with these corpses?" he asked me several times. He was inordinately vexed by the whole thing and during one such conversation, while we were having dinner together, he suddenly fainted. Afterward he said to me that he was convinced that all this chatter about corpses meant I had death-wishes towards him. I was more than surprised by this interpretation. I was alarmed by the intensity of his fantasies—so strong that, obviously, they could cause him to faint. (1961, 156)

Freud's interpretation is perhaps supported by Jung's confusion about the locality of the peat-bog corpses, which were not in Bremen at all. Jung states ingenuously, and not like an analyst, that he had thought about them "when we were in Bremen, but being a bit muddled, confused them with the mummies in the lead cellars of that city" (1961, 156).

Here is Jung's version of the second attack at Munich in 1912. It is fascinating that in his account of the argument about the significance of the son's erasing the name of the father, he completely failed to mention the name of Karl Abraham. And the name of this brother-figure with whom he was in conflict is not mentioned anywhere in "Father Abraham's" autobiography:

> Someone had turned the conversation to Amenophis IV [Ikhnaton]. The point was made that as a result of his negative attitude towards his father he had destroyed his father's cartouches on the steles, and that at the back of his great creation of a monotheistic religion there lurked a father complex. This sort of thing irritated me, and I attempted to argue that Amenophis had been a creative and profoundly religious person whose acts could not be explained by personal resistances towards his father. On the contrary, I said, he had held the memory of his father in honor, and his zeal for destruction had been

directed only against the name of the god Amon, which he had everywhere annihilated. (1961, 137)

Jung goes on to describe how Freud slid off his chair in a faint:

Everyone clustered helplessly around him. I picked him up, carried him into the next room and laid him on a sofa. [This recalls Freud's Egyptian dream of his mother being carried— here Freud himself is the mummy.] As I was carrying him, he half came to, and I shall never forget the look he cast at me. In his weakness he looked at me as if I were his father. Whatever causes may have contributed to this faint—the atmosphere was very tense—the fantasy of father-murder was common to both cases. (1961, 157)

Freud analyzed his own fainting attacks and came to two conclusions that he mentioned to Jones. One was that all "his attacks could be traced to the effect on him of his young brother's (Julius's) death when [Freud] was a year and seven months old" (Jones 1953, 317). I have already mentioned that in association to his "non vixit" dream, Freud talks of the far-reaching consequences of his fulfilled death wishes toward Julius and the "germ of guilt" (Freud 1960, 219) that remained. Wilhelm Fliess was the current embodiment of Julius at the time of the "non vixit" dream. Jones (1953) said that shortly after the Munich attack of November 1912 Freud wrote him an explanation:

"It was a repetition". . . he wrote to me: "I cannot forget that six and four years ago I suffered from very similar though not such intense symptoms *in the same room* of the Park Hotel. I saw Munich first when I visited Fliess during his illness and this town seems to have acquired a strong connexion with my relation to that man. There is some piece of unruly homosexual feeling at the root of the matter." (317; my italics)

Jung, then, was the revenant of Fliess as part of a father/son confrontation, as in his previous fainting fit at Munich.

Jones continues,

I visited Freud in Vienna a month after this and my memory is that he told me that the final quarrel with Fliess took place in the same room. But I cannot completely vouch for this point since it is possible that he only said that the room was associated with Fliess, which it certainly was. (317)

Freud's fainting apparently involved both sides of the Oedipus complex: punishment for death wishes toward rivals for the exclusive possession of the mother, and homosexuality associated with passive surrender to them—in short, the basic bisexuality of the human being, here linked with the person whose *name* he had once forgotten in the struggle to claim originality for discovery of the concept: Fliess.

I am going to go back in time at this point to interpolate Abraham's meeting with Fliess (in 1911), before he wrote to Freud about his Amenhotep paper (in 1912).

Freud had an intense neurotic and dependent relationship to Fliess from 1887 to 1902 (when Freud was aged thirty-one to forty-six); Jones (1953) calls it "a passionate friendship for someone intellectually his inferior" (287), to whom he subordinated his judgment and opinions. Jones finds "extraordinary in the highest degree" (287) the contrast between this subordination and the liberating pioneer effort of Freud's self-analysis (which was, however, carried out in part by making use of Fliess as auxiliary analyst). The two men met for the last time in 1900, their correspondence broke off in 1902, and in 1906 there was an irreparable break when Fliess attacked Freud publicly in a nasty pamphlet for having furnished information about Fliess's views on bisexuality to others. The charge was not without foundation; the conflict over priority in relation to bisexuality was still affecting Freud. Freud felt that the publication of his private apologetic letters to Fliess was unforgivable, and he obviously considered the tone of Fliess's attack as revealing paranoia. He replied in 1906 with two angry letters to the press, characterizing Fliess as ambitious and overbearing. That was the end of the relationship.

Although Freud felt that he had largely freed himself from his dependence on Fliess (see the renunciatory letter of March 23, 1900 [Freud 1954, 313–14]), the separation left a scar. Part of the price we pay for the closeness and identification with others that nourish our identity is that we are left with psychic conflicts involving them and with qualities and aspects of character and pathology both like them and evoked by them that may not be what we want. Freud's fainting fits show the conflict. The residual Fliess-like qualities include Freud's continuing (although greatly diminished) interest in periodicity and even numerology (Fliess's passion)—although it is clear that he was aware of the pathological basis for Fliess's preoccupation with numbers.

When Abraham set up his practice of psychoanalysis in Berlin in 1907 (a year after Fliess and Freud had quarreled publicly over bisexuality), he asked Freud for referrals. Freud replied,

> That you have my sympathy and best wishes in setting out on your new path is obvious, and if possible I should like to offer you more than that. If my close friendship with Dr. Fliess of Berlin still existed, the way would be levelled for you, but now unfortunately the road is completely blocked. (Freud and Abraham 1965, 9)

Fliess was a very popular and successful medical practitioner in Berlin. Abraham was aware of what had passed between the two older men, and in 1911 he wrote a letter which involved sharing an idea of Fliess, almost asking for Freud's permission to meet him:

> At the moment I find myself in a dilemma. The other day I mentioned to a colleague that I had, in a case of circular psychosis, been struck by the appearance of masculine and feminine periods. [These are Fliess's concepts.] She spoke of this to Fliess, with whom she is friendly, and a few days later told me of Fliess's request that I should visit him. (Freud and Abraham 1965, 99)

This request involved a contact with Fliess for Freud by way of Abraham; and the appeal this had for Freud may have motivated him to an immediate (impatient) reply to Abraham's letter, which he marked "in haste":

> I am replying by return of post because of what you say about Fliess, and am taking the liberty of giving you my advice unasked, that is, telling you my attitude in the matter. I cannot see why you should not call on him. In the first place you will meet a remarkable, indeed fascinating man, and on the other hand you will perhaps have an opportunity of getting scientifically closer to the grain of truth that is *surely* contained in his theory of periodicity, a possibility that is denied to me for personal reasons. He will certainly try to sidetrack you from psychoanalysis (and, as he thinks, from me) and to guide you into his own channel. But I am sure you will not *betray* both of us to him. You know his complex, and are aware that I am the centre of it, and so you will be able to evade it. You know in advance that he is a hard man, which I took years to discover. (Freud and Abraham 1965, 100–01; my italics)

Freud's impatience to reply shows the same level of excitement—
the mixture of longing, desire, and anger[10]—that was present when
Freud "penetrated into" his parents' bedroom and, not being able
to control his urine (not being able to wait), evoked the unforgettable reproach that I have taken for the title of this book. "Looking
on" at the contact of Abraham and Fliess in his mind's eye evoked
Freud's impatience (and expectation of betrayal), originally called
up by primal-scene memories and fantasies.

Two weeks later Abraham describes the meeting:

> Now I must tell you about Fliess. I had a very friendly recep-
> tion. He refrained from any attacks on Vienna; he has closed
> his mind to the new results of psychoanalysis since the conflict,
> but showed great interest in all I told him. I did not get the
> fascinating impression that you predicted.[11] Fliess may have
> changed in the last few years but nevertheless, I did get the
> impression of a penetrating and original thinker. In my opinion
> he lacks real greatness, and this is borne out in his scientific work.
> He starts off with some valuable ideas, but all further work is
> concentrated merely on proving their correctness and on their
> more exact formulation. He met me without prejudice, has
> meanwhile visited me in turn, and I must admit that he made
> no attempt to draw me over to his side in the way you feared. I
> have learned many interesting things from him, and am glad to
> have made his acquaintance, perhaps the most valuable I could
> make among colleagues in Berlin. (Freud and Abraham 1965,
> 103)

To this cool and seemingly objective appraisal Freud replied,

> You must not think Fliess so crude as to betray any intention
> in the first hour. Unfortunately he is the opposite, subtle or even

10. Robert Fliess (the psychoanalyst son of Wilhelm) has called impatience "the
cannibalistic affect." The theme of Freud's impatience with delay in sending and
receiving letters is intimately linked with Fliess and emerges again in relation to
Jung—see next chapter.

11. Jones (1953) mentions this letter of Abraham's in his description of Fliess:
"Of those who knew him, with the exception of the level-headed Karl Abraham,
who was not impressed, everyone speaks of his 'fascinating personality'" (289; my
italics). This is a distortion based on only part of what Abraham said after the first
meeting, and it leaves out the evolution of Abraham's opinion away from "level-
headedness" and toward "fascination," which will be followed below.

cunning. You will certainly come across his complex. Do not forget that it was through him that both of us came to understand the secret of Paranoia. . . . What you say about his work strikes me as remarkably true: I once loved him very much and therefore overlooked a good deal. (Freud and Abraham 1965, 103)

Fliess then disappears from the correspondence, which goes on to deal with the quarrels about Jung, and then, in January of 1912, with Abraham's Ikhnaton paper. By 1913, after the fainting episode at Munich, Freud was able to see the depth not only of Jung's rebelliousness but of his disturbance, as he had with Fliess's. He wrote Abraham, "Jung is crazy, but I have no desire for a separation and should like to let him wreck himself first" (Freud and Abraham, 1965, 141). Freud pays tribute to Abraham as a *Menschenkenner:* "Since being taken in by Jung, my confidence in my practical judgment has greatly declined" (141).

Later, in 1914, Jung resigned as president of the International Psycho-Analytical Association, and Freud proposed that Abraham take his place. Grotjahn (1968) says, "As had his biblical namesake, he accepted his fate" (9). Freud then wrote to Abraham,

So we are at last rid of them, the brutal,[12] sanctimonious Jung and his disciples. I must thank you for the vast amount of trouble, *the exceptional clear-sightedness,* with which you supported me and our common cause. All my life I have been looking for friends who would not *betray* me, and now, not far from its natural end, I hope I have found them. (1965, 186; my italics)

The last-quoted sentence is again reminiscent of the "non vixit" dream of 1898, in which he talked of his relationship with his nephew John, two friends who "made complaints about" (that is, *betrayed*) each other, as a prototype of the urge to reproduce "the ideal situation of childhood [so] that friend and enemy . . . come together in a single individual" (1900b, 483). In 1898, the single individual was Wilhelm Fliess. In 1914, Jung had become a revenant of Fliess for Freud.

In this letter Freud praises Abraham for his clear-sightedness.[13]

12. Freud had used this word in 1906 to characterize Fliess when referring to the latter's pamphlet on bisexuality, which he described as a result of "the overbearing presumption of a *brutal* personality" (Jones 1953, 316; my italics).

13. I presented a short version of this chapter at the meetings of the American

He had need to use Abraham's eyes, undazzled by the sun, as auxiliaries of his own. ("You are requested / To close the eyes," his dream following his father's death had said.) Thus it was of special importance to Freud that Abraham share his view of Fliess. Tragically, as Abraham became ill and finally dependent on Fliess as his physician, his view of Fliess was that of Freud at the height of his neurotic dependence.

Abraham served in the German army in the First World War. He contracted chronic bronchitis and went to Wilhelm Fliess as a patient. Grotjahn comments, "[Abraham] always maintained that Fliess sent him the most suitable cases for psychoanalysis, and his trust in Wilhelm Fliess as a capable diagnostician endured to Abraham's last illness" (1968, 3). Freud, too, had been a patient of Fliess and even had his nose operated on by him on several occasions. When Freud became ill in 1923, there is evidence of the revival of the wish to be treated by Fliess.

Freud noticed trouble with his jaw in February of 1923, and in April an operation was performed to remove a growth. It turned out to be cancerous, and this illness was to torment Freud for the rest of his life and finally to kill him. The first operation in 1923 was terrible—Freud nearly bled to death—and it was followed by x-ray and radium treatment. Although Freud was not at first told that he had cancer, he knew it. A few months after the operation, Freud's beloved grandson Heinz (Heinele) died. This was the only time (Jones says) that Freud was seen to shed tears, and he said that he found the blow unbearable, much worse than his own cancer. In September 1923, a much more radical operation was

---

Psychoanalytic Association in December 1971. I am indebted to Dr. Richard Sterba, my discussant on that occasion, for pointing out to me that the English translation of this passage from the letter of July 26, 1914, does not correspond to the German text as printed in *Sigmund Freud/Karl Abraham Briefe, 1907–1926* (Frankfurt am Main: S. Fischer Verlag, 1965). Specifically, the key words "extraordinary clear-sightedness" are the translator's (Hilde Abraham's) rendition of "ausserordentliche zielbewusste Tätigkeit"; the literal meaning, "extraordinary methodical activity," has nothing to do with imagery involving the eye (although it can be connected with Freud's view of Abraham as "too Prussian"). I would assume that the German version is correct, although one could be sure only by checking the original letter. I have not rewritten the passage since it is still true that Freud used Abraham to supplement his eyes in his role as a *Menschenkenner,* but the moral should be drawn that any student of Freud who does not know German thoroughly and who works from another language is not necessarily the most "clear-sighted" guide to Freud's use of imagery.

performed, and it became necessary for him to wear a painful prosthesis over his palate.

Just before the cancer was found, there was an exchange of letters between Abraham and Freud which again touches on Egypt and Ikhnaton. The occasion was the much-publicized discovery of the tomb of Ikhnaton's successor, Tutankhamen. Abraham had sent a number of newspaper clippings about it to Freud, who replied (March 4, 1923), "It now seems certain that they will soon find the mummy of the king and perhaps also that of his consort, a daughter of *our analytic* Pharaoh" (1965, 334; my italics). There was no amnesia of Abraham's paper in 1923. In his reply, Abraham seriously proposed that they visit Egypt together the following summer. Freud answered that he was "neither rich nor well enough," adding, ominously, "You must gradually get used to the idea of my mortality and frailty" (365).

Another worry for Freud at this time was the behavior of Otto Rank, behavior that involved "betrayal" (and might have been brought on by Rank's reaction to Freud's illness). Abraham found himself again in the difficult position of criticizing a beloved disciple of Freud, pushing Freud toward an undesired loss. Abraham wrote that he felt forced

> to my deepest sorrow, and not for the first time in the 20 years of my analytic life, to sound a warning. . . . [We see] the manifestations of a regression in the scientific field, the symptoms of which agree in every small detail with those of Jung's secession from psychoanalysis. . . . Do you remember that at the first Congress in Salzburg I warned you about Jung? At that time you dismissed my fears and assumed my motive was jealousy. Another Salzburg Congress is before us and once more I come to you in the same role—a role I would rather not play. (1965, 349)

Indeed, all was repeated, Freud was once more angry with the messenger, accusing Abraham of stirring up trouble. To a letter from Freud expressing this, Abraham responded,

> Your letter expresses a distrust of me that I find extremely painful, and, at the same time, strange. . . . I must state that your letter has not evoked even a shadow of guilt in me. . . . I [knew] I was exposing myself to a similar reaction from you as in the past, when I drew your attention to unwelcome facts . . . now the reaction has set in after all. (356)

Again Abraham turned out to be correct, and things were set to
rights between the two men after Abraham had once more drawn
down on himself the anger focused on those who play the role of
Teiresias, teller of unwelcome truth.

Later in 1924, there is a strange sequence of letters in which
numerology—Fliess's obsession (he thought that in relation to what
he called the "masculine" number 23 and the "feminine" number
28 he had found the secret of all periodicity in life)—became the
topic for Freud and Abraham. Freud was ill and very much aware
of his cancerous condition. He felt, as he had a year previously,
that his (sixty-eighth) birthday might be his last. Abraham, in an
unpublished letter of April 26, 1924, had mentioned his intention
to carry out a study of the significance of the number 7 in myths
and customs (he never did). Freud referred to this in a letter of
August 1924:

> In re 7: I am putting at your disposal an idea the value of
> which I cannot judge myself because of *ignorance*. I should like
> to take a historical view and believe that the significance of the
> number 7 originated in a period when men counted in sixes.
> (Here *ignorance* sets in.) In that case seven would not be the last
> of a series as it is now in the week, but the first of a second series
> and, like first things, subject to taboo. The fact that the initial
> number of the third series, that is to say 13, is the unluckiest of
> all numbers would fit in with this. The origin of my idea was a
> remark in a history of Assyria that 19 was also one of the suspect
> numbers, which the author explains with reference to the length
> of the month by the equation $30 + 19 = 49$, or 7×7. However,
> $19 = 13 + 6$, the beginning of a fourth series of sixes. This
> system of sixes would thus be pre-astronomical. One should
> investigate what is known of such a system, of which enough
> traces remain (dozen, gross, division of the circle into 360 de-
> grees). Moreover, it is notable how many prime numbers appear
> in this series: 1, 7, 13, 19, 25 is an exception but is followed by
> 31, 37, 43, 49, which is again 7×7. (1965, 365; my italics)

Here Freud seems almost to be consciously parodying Fliess, but
that is obviously not the case. Freud sounds so much like Fliess that
I postulate that a longing to be taken care of by his old doctor is
expressed by way of an identification with him. The last sentence
of the letter shows awareness of the link to Fliess: "The craziest
things can be done with numbers so be careful." Alongside this

identification, Freud would appear to be warning Abraham here to beware of Fliess.

There had come a time in Freud's relations with Fliess when he could no longer believe in his friend's mathematical juggling and chose, rather than to quarrel, to disclaim knowledge (or proclaim ignorance, as in the above letter). Kris (1954) writes about Freud's reactions during those years before the two men parted:

The less the observed facts fitted in with [Fliess's] theoretical requirements, the more strained became his calculations. So long as the time intervals in which he dealt could be explained as parts or multiples of 23 and 28, Freud followed him, but Fliess soon found himself obliged to explain the intervals with which he was confronted by combinations of four figures and to use not only 23 and 28 but 5 (28 − 23) and 51 (28 + 23). Freud refused to accompany him in this step, excusing himself on the ground of his lack of mathematical knowledge. (10)

When Fliess in 1901 wrote Freud accusing him of not believing in the period theories, Freud had apologetically replied,

You know that I lack the slightest mathematical ability. [I am] a friend who because of his ignorance can never be dangerous. (1954, 336)

For Freud the number 7 had specific associations with Fliess. When he had been a believer in Fliess's period theories, Freud would ask him about the future, almost as if he were consulting a numerologist/fortune teller. In 1899, Freud wrote Fliess about a current dearth of productive work: "According to an earlier calculation of yours, 1900–1901 ought to be a productive period for me (every *seven*-and a half years)" (1954, 300–01). On January 8, 1900, Freud reproached Fliess for not writing sooner: "Now do not let another long interval like this happen again (Dec. 24th–Jan. 7th = 14 = 28/2)" (1954, 308). Here Freud's longing for Fliess was expressed in terms of parts of the feminine period number 28, which involves a series of seven. The longing for Fliess was an expression of the passive, "feminine" aspect of Freud's nature and of the homosexual striving to which he ascribed his fainting fits in the presence of Fliess and then Jung. (Freud to Fliess [May 7 (!), 1900]: "No one can replace the intercourse with a friend that a particular—perhaps feminine—side of me requires" [1954, 302].)

In 1913, after the fainting fit in Munich in 1912 ("How sweet

. . . to die"), Freud wrote a numerologic letter to Ferenczi which again expresses a wish for Fliess (probably now reinforced by wishes to keep Jung). Freud was about to make another visit to Munich. One sees how much he still holds with the period theory and how important 7 is. The occasion of the letter is Ferenczi's fortieth birthday:

> Your *nostalgic* letter moved me very much, first because it reminded me of my own 40th birthday, since when [1896] I have changed my skin several times, which as we know, occurs every *seven* years. At that time I had reached the peak of loneliness, had lost my old friends and hadn't acquired any new ones.[14] No one paid any attention to me and the only thing that kept me going was a bit of defiance and the beginning of the Interpretation of Dreams. . . . Abraham is to visit us at the end of August and will probably accompany us to Munich. Your hope of my being able to tell you something new by then I cannot as yet support. My good ideas actually *occur in 7 year cycles:* in 1891 I started work on aphasia; 1898/9, the interpretation of dreams; 1904/5, with its relation to the unconscious; 1911/12, totem and tabu; thus I am probably in the waning stage and won't be able to count on anything of importance before 1918/19 (provided the chain doesn't break before). (1960, 300; my italics)

In this resurgence of numerology, Freud is identifying with Fliess instead of remembering him or longing for him. The year of Freud's fortieth birthday, 1896, was also the year his father died. In a letter of October 26, 1896, informing Fliess of Jacob Freud's death, Freud wrote,

> Yesterday we buried the old man, who died during the night of October 13. . . . The last attack was followed by pulmonary edema and quite an easy death. All of it happened in my critical period, and I am really quite down because of it. (1985, 201)[15]

I think that following his cancer operation, the death of his grandson Heinz, and the loss of another "analytic" son (Rank), there was an intensification for Freud of the conflicting wishes to kill and replace the father and to submit to him, with the attendant

14. In this last statement, Freud has eliminated Fliess! This is astonishing. The friendship was in full flower in 1896.

15. In his translation, Masson has the following footnote: "Fliess, in *Der Ablauf*

expectation of castration and death. The losses of the "sons" could have been regarded as punishment for the death wishes against the father and brothers. Much of Freud's conflict with his father was (as it generally is) displaced onto his more dispensable and less dangerous siblings. For Freud this had begun with Julius and John and Phillip, culminating in Fliess. Fliess continued to have the power to appear as a revenant of the beloved and hated brothers and father of the past. Freud's illness and suffering in the years before Abraham's death in 1925 made for an upsurge of regressive passive feeling which the indomitable man was fighting successfully and heroically in his behavior and in his continuing power of creative thinking. But the longing for Fliess must have been fed by the tragic illness of another "son" and younger brother-figure— Karl Abraham—and by Abraham's increasing involvement with and passive surrender to Fliess.

According to Schur (1969), there was a similar period in 1904, following the beginning of the quarrel with Fliess over priority in the idea of bisexuality. This led to the disturbance on the Acropolis with its fainting-like episode and was also connected with a Fliess-inspired preoccupation with numbers. As documentation, Schur quotes the following letter to Jung, written in 1909, about the year 1904:

> Some years ago [1904] I discovered that I had the conviction I would die between the ages of 61–62, which was then a long way off. . . . At that time I went with my brother to Greece. It was really uncanny how the numbers 61 or 62, in conjunction with 1 or 2, kept appearing under all kinds of circumstances. . . . Being in low spirits I hoped to breathe easier when a room on the first floor of our Athens hotel was assigned to us. There 61 was out of the question. Well, I got room 31 (with fatalistic licence, after all, half of 61–62), and this smarter and more nimble number proved to be more persistent in its persecution

---

des Lebens, writes: 'Prof. Sigmund Freud in Vienna at one time advised me of the dates of his father's life:

$$\left.\begin{array}{l} \text{born April 1, 1815} \\[1em] \text{died Oct. 24, 1896} \end{array}\right\} \quad 29{,}792 = 38 \times 28^2$$

Freud senior was born on the same day as Bismarck, who died on July 30, 1898, therefore lived exactly $644 = 23 \times 28$ days longer'" (2d ed., 142) [1985, 201].

than the first one. . . . Because there *are* areas in my system where I am just thirsty for knowledge and not at all superstitious, I have since attempted an analysis, and here it is. It all began in the year 1899, when two events occurred simultaneously: first I wrote *The Interpretation of Dreams* and second, I was assigned a new telephone number which I still have—14362. A connection between the two could easily be established: in the year 1899, when I wrote *The Interpretation of Dreams*, I was *43* years old. What more natural then [*sic*] that the other numbers referred to the end of my life, namely 61 or 62. Suddenly there was method in the madness. The superstition that I would die between 61–62 showed itself to be the equivalent of a conviction that I had fulfilled my life's work with *The Interpretation of Dreams*, didn't have to produce anything further, and could die in peace. You will admit that with this knowledge the thing no longer sounds so absurd. By the way, there is a hidden influence of Fliess in all this; it was in the year of his attack that the superstition erupted. (1969, 28–29)

Schur says the preoccupation with numbers "had the character and intensity of a severe compulsive symptom" (29).

Relevant to this is another meaning of *seven* for Freud that is furnished by Jones. On the night before the final decision about whether he would receive a travel grant (which he did get and used to study with Charcot) in 1885,

Freud dreamed that his representative, who was none other than Brücke, told him he had no chance because there were *seven* other applicants with more favorable prospects. Since there had been seven brothers and sisters besides himself in the family it is not hard to perceive the reassurance in this simple little dream. (Jones 1953, 75–76)

An enigmatic use of *seven* comes up in a letter to Ferenczi of 1921, quoted by Jones. It links *seven* with the prediction of death and shows the ability to transcend the temptation connected with superstition (that was associated for Freud with Fliess and with Jung):

On March 13th of this year I quite suddenly took a step into real old age. Since then the thought of death has not left me, and sometimes I have the impression that *seven* of my internal

organs are fighting to have the honor of bringing my life to an
end. . . . Still I have not succumbed to this hypochondria, but
view it quite coolly. (Jones 1957, 79; my italics)

Schur (1964) feels that Freud was paraphrasing the Greek pentam-
eter that goes, "Seven cities are competing for the honor of being
the birthplace of Homer." This is convincing; by evoking it Freud
would be equating birth with death. If we follow Jones's equation
of *seven* with Freud's siblings, the death wishes against the seven
sisters and brothers whose birth followed his (especially the fulfilled
ones against Julius) and the retaliation for those wishes might be
involved in Freud's fanciful paraphrase of a Greek original. If so,
another *seven* may be relevant, Aeschylus's *Seven against Thebes,* with
its fratricidal theme.

There was a numerologic mystery that concerned Freud for a
good part of his creative life: the riddle of the Theban Sphinx.
Graves states it thus:

"What being, with only one voice, has sometimes two feet,
sometimes three, sometimes four, and is weakest when it has the
most?" Oedipus' answer: "Man—because he crawls on all fours
as an infant, stands firmly on his feet as a youth, and leans on a
staff in his old age." (1955, 10)

Freud interpreted this as "the great riddle of where babies come
from which is perhaps the first problem to engage a child's mental
powers" (1909b, 133), thereby connecting it with the child's sexual
curiosity. With his interpretation Freud transformed instinct-rid-
den numerologic superstition to psychic analysis. The sublimation
of the sexual wish to see and know into a passion to understand
was so much a part of Freud's mastery that his followers were
inspired to present him with a medallion of Oedipus reading the
riddle of the Sphinx, underlining Freud's identification with
Oedipus.[16]

On October 25, 1924, Abraham wrote the final communication
between the two men on the number 7, in which he dismisses
Freud's half-serious historico-numerologic suggestions, substituting

16. The Sphinx was a creature derived from Egypt and was bisexual—part of
its mystery is the mystery of bisexuality. Elsewhere I have written of the Sphinx as
representing the bisexual primal parent (see Shengold 1963). The Sphinx also has
been seen as an image of the parents in intercourse.

a speculative psychological (yet still faintly Fliess-like) explanation that involves the Oedipus complex and the riddle of the Sphinx:

The investigation into the number seven has been completely put aside for the time being. . . . I see that one cannot attack the problem either from the angle of astronomical significance or from that of numerical systems. The basic psychological phenomenon seems to me to lie in the ambivalent attitude of mankind to the number seven. This must represent the thing to which one is most ambivalent and I thus come back once more to the Oedipus complex. Seven is the number of abstinence (Sabbath, etc.) everywhere, it expresses the taboo and is at the same time the number of many rites compulsively performed. I see in this double significance the justification for assuming a fusion of two other numbers in this one, and believe that the significance of the three equalling father and the four equalling mother (three patriarchs and four matriarchs mentioned in the Bible etc.) will have to be retained.

The numerological letters about 7 prefigure the fateful reappearance of Fliess in the correspondence between Freud and Abraham. Eight months after the sensible letter representing a repudiation of the "Fliessian" approach to number 7, Abraham became ill. In a letter of June 7, 1925, he complained of a persistent feverish bronchitis. This had started with an injury to the pharynx caused by a fishbone. It went on to a septic bronchopneumonia, lung abscess, and finally to a terminal subphrenic abscess. The illness "took the typical course of septicaemia prior to the introduction of antibiotics, with swinging temperatures, remission and euphoria. Abraham's previous emphysema had doubtless made him susceptible to such infection" (Freud and Abraham 1965, 382, editor's note). The euphoria implies mental disturbances that might account for Abraham's adherence to Fliess and his systems, which became part of the pathological dependence of a dying man on his physician.

Freud continued to worry about Abraham's health, and the two compared illnesses, Freud noting the twenty-one-year age difference between them. On September 8, 1925, Abraham wrote that he had been exhausted and euphoric (he speaks of a "new manic phase"): "I shall in any case have to undergo some treatment for my nose and throat from Fliess. If this letter were not already unduly long, I would tell you *how my illness has most strikingly confirmed all Fliess's views on periodicity*" (1925, 395, my italics).[17] Freud must have been appalled by this: because of his concern about what was going on in Abraham, in mind and body, and because he had more than once had *his* nose treated by Fliess when *he* had believed in Fliess. Abraham was identifying with Fliess!

In his short reply to this letter, Freud simply expressed his concern about Abraham's continuing illness. Several weeks later, Abraham wrote about his worry over Freud's health. He himself was feeling

> very much better. . . . I am so sorry to hear that you are continuously troubled by certain discomforts. . . . I have been wondering whether a stay in a very dry climate might be beneficial. But I do not know whether you still need to be near your surgeon. You may be interested to hear that Fliess, who heard about your illness two years ago, has repeatedly asked after your health with warmest interest. As far as I am concerned I must repeat here once again that I owe him the utmost gratitude. (1965, 397)

Abraham here contrasts Freud's relationship to his surgeon, Pichler—in whose near presence Freud was obliged to remain— with Abraham's relationship to Freud's old surgeon, Fliess, whose care deserves Abraham's "utmost gratitude." Fliess is portrayed as warm and interested in Freud. In this letter Abraham sounds euphoric.

The final exchange of letters concerns a strange conflict over the project of a commercial film to be made under psychoanalytic auspices (it was finally filmed under the title *Secret of the Soul*). Abraham supported the idea, but Freud was very reluctant, and others objected strongly, expressing themselves and behaving in a way that Abraham disapproved of. Freud again accused the younger man of intolerance (apparently this was one of the times Freud found him "too Prussian"). But the unfortunate acerbity of the last letter must also have to do with unconscious rivalry for the other Berliner (and Prussian), Fliess. A film project called Secret of the

17. One wants at first to feel that this last statement is not meant straightforwardly but is rather sarcasm dryly directed at Fliess. That kind of humor (which Jung might have used) would not be characteristic of Abraham, and his next-quoted letter, as usual direct and serious, seems to me to rule out the slight possibility of Abraham's mocking Fliess.

Soul would inevitably connect with the eyes and the forbidden, invoking Oedipus and the Sphinx and the riddle. Abraham wrote,

> You know, dear Professor, that I am very unwilling to enter once again into a discussion of the film affair. But because of your reproach of harshness (in your circular letter), I find myself once more in the same position as on several previous occasions. In almost twenty years, we have had no differences of opinion except where personalities were concerned whom I, very much to my regret, had to criticize. The same sequence of events repeated itself each time: *you indulgently overlooked everything that could be challenged* in the behavior of the persons concerned, whilst all the blame—which you subsequently recognized as unjustified—was directed against me. In Jung's case your criticism was that of "jealousy"; in the case of Rank "unfriendly behavior" and, this time, "harshness." Could the sequence of events not be the same once again: *I advanced an opinion which is basically yours as well but which you did not admit into consciousness.* All the unpleasure linked to the relevant facts is then turned against the person who had drawn attention to them. (1965, 398; my italics)

Abraham here again speaks as "the analyst" who tells the patient to open his eyes to unwelcome truth; but there is another meaning in the italicized words. Abraham had been advancing his favorable opinion of Fliess which Freud consciously did not, and did not want to, share—but which was still present as part of Freud's unconscious longing. It is not surprising that this conflictuous counterpoint brought out in Freud's final letter to Abraham the "harshness" with which he had charged Abraham. It must be remembered that Freud had no idea that Abraham was dying and that he was writing him a last letter:

> Dear Friend,
>
> I note with pleasure that your illness has not changed you in any way, and am willing to regard you as having again recovered. That takes a great load off my mind.
>
> It does not make a deep impression on me that I cannot convert myself to your point of view in the film affair. There are a good many things that I see differently and judge differently.
>
> Let us not give too much play to repetition compulsion. You were certainly right about Jung, and not quite so right about

Rank. That matter took a different course, and would have passed over more easily if it had not been taken so very seriously in Berlin. It is still quite possible that you may be even less right in the matter with which we are concerned now. You are not necessarily always right. But should you turn out to be right this time too, nothing would prevent me from once again admitting it.

With that let us close the argument about something that you yourself describe as a trifle. Such differences of opinion can never be avoided, but only quickly overcome.

What matters more to me is to hear whether you intend to stay in Berlin or spend the winter in a milder climate. I am not quite sure in my mind what to wish for you, but in any case let the outcome be that you cause us no more worry.

With cordial greetings to you and your wife and children.

Yours,

Freud. (1965, 399)

Abraham died on December 25, 1925, at the age of forty-eight. Freud wrote to Abraham's widow:

Since my telegram on receiving the news of your husband's death I have put off writing to you. It was too difficult, and I hoped it would become easier. Then I fell ill myself, became feverish, and have not yet recovered. But I already see that putting it off was useless, it is just as difficult now as it was then. I have no substitute for him, and no consolatory words for you that would be anything new. That we have to submit with resignation to the blows of fate you know already; and you will have guessed that to me his loss is particularly painful because, with the selfishness of old age, I think he could easily have been spared for the probable short duration of my own life. (1965, 399)

The death was, he wrote to Jones,

perhaps the greatest blow that could have struck us. Who would have thought when we were all together in the Harz that he would be the first to leave this senseless life! We must work on and hold together. No one can replace the personal loss, but for the work no one must be irreplaceable. I shall soon fall out—it is to be hoped that the others will do so only much later—but

the work must be continued, in comparison with whose dimen-
sions we are all equally small. (Jones 1955, 364)

The loss was another great blow for Freud—part of a gauntlet
of fate that he was traversing. His letters to Mrs. Abraham and
Jones have the characteristic heroic, oedipean note of the man who
can confront *Ananke,* bitter Necessity. And he was able to go on—to
fifteen more years of creative work of the highest order, defying
cancer, old age, and finally the Nazis, who drove him out of the
land as Moses had been driven out of Egypt.

This chapter has resembled a detective story—the mystery being
why Freud erased from his mind Karl Abraham's name and his
paper on Amenhotep when, many years after the younger man's
death, the old man wrote *Moses and Monotheism.* The answer I have
suggested is that Abraham had become another of the beloved and
hated ghosts that haunted and had become part of Freud's mind,
victims of his death wishes. The most important of these were
Freud's father and his younger brother Julius. The transference
was accomplished mainly by way of Abraham's association with the
chief reincarnation of all for Freud's adult life: Wilhelm Fliess.
Even after Freud's break with him, Fliess continued to evoke a
concentrate of wishes attached to the important people from
Freud's childhood—father, mother, brother. This kind of transference permitted Freud to make use of Fliess as an analyst-figure
during his self-analysis. Abraham too sometimes played the part of
an analyst for Freud, pointing out unwelcome truths and urging
renunciation. Freud's transference was most powerfully enhanced
by a kind of unconscious projection: Freud could see in Abraham
the magical, worshipful dependence on Fliess that he had consciously suppressed and did not want to be part of himself. These
essentially homosexual feelings would produce rage toward both
Berliners, especially painful for Freud toward the sick Abraham,
who was so much wanted and so vulnerable. Both Abraham and
Fliess drew on themselves the death wishes directed toward the
parent-analyst as well as those displaced onto the rival sibling. Both
were sometimes unconsciously replaced by or merged into such
biblical and historical figures as Abraham, Moses, Joseph, Goethe,
and Mephistopheles.

The first and greatest of detective stories, *Oedipus Rex,* is involved, as are all the motive forces expressed in the Family Ro-

mance fantasy.[18] We know from Freud's dream of his dead mother when he was seven (!) and from his lifelong identifications with Joseph and Moses that Freud's family complexes were expressed and lived out in metaphors derived from the Bible and from Egypt. In attempting to write a Family Romance of the Jews, to find them another and an Egyptian father, thereby permitting Moses (and Freud as Moses) to be the child of a princess, Freud was dismissing Father Abraham and his namesake, Karl Abraham. The beloved and lost disciple is forgotten insofar as he is connected with Egypt, the Bible, and the oedipal struggle between father and son over the body of the mother, which is the essence of the story of Amenhotep IV.

But perhaps the most basic answer to the puzzle involves the interplay between murder and passive wishes and the castration complex in relation to the revenants. Death wishes toward the father evoke submission to the father. This vicious cycle—seeking castration to avoid castration, engendering hatred while trying to escape hatred—was called by Freud, in *Analysis Terminable and Interminable* (1937), a work written after *Moses and Monotheism,* the bedrock beyond which analysis cannot go: "The attitude proper to the opposite sex which has succumbed to repression . . . the repudiation of femininity [that] can be nothing else than a biological fact, a part of the great riddle of sex" (1937, 250, 252). We come again to the riddle of the Sphinx and are back full circle to Fliess and the concept of bisexuality, which evoked so much conflict and rage and was the subject of Freud's first publicly acknowledged erasing of a name.

The juxtaposition of incest and sex in the Oedipus complex and its attendant castration complex has supplied a ground bass for this chapter against which various themes have appeared, faded, and reappeared like leitmotifs: Abraham and Moses (two of Freud's alter egos or ego ideals); Israel and Egypt; betrayal; the struggle

18. Freud believed the Family Romance to be a universal unconscious fantasy that often is the subject of conscious daydream. The child feels that he or she is not the offspring of the apparent actual parents but has been stolen away from the real wonderful (royal, noble, famous, gifted, etc.) ones—idealized creatures who would supply idealized love and banish conflict, hatred, and deficiency. I regard the Family Romance as an expression of narcissistic defense (regressive idealization) in relation to preoedipal and oedipal dangers of conflicts (in the mind and in reality) between the self and the parents.

for succession; numerology and superstition; the sun and sight; Prussianism and brutality—these are subjects for Freud that, to continue the musical analogy, combine polyphonically while reflecting and expressing the theme present in the ground bass. Listening for themes and patterns in the form of metaphors is part of the art of psychoanalysis (see Kanzer 1958, 1969) although the music there is, so to speak, for two players. In this and other chapters, I have tried to portray the counterpoint of Freud's living out his passionate involvements in the events and characters of the Old Testament stories that had absorbed him so early and provided him with so many figures whom he could use to disguise and amplify his identity.

7

FREUD, GOETHE, JUNG,
AND THE DEVIL

To live with someone and to live in someone are
two fundamentally different matters. There are
people in whom one can live without living with
them, and vice versa. To combine both requires the
purest degree of love and friendship.

—Goethe

Johann Eckermann, Goethe's Boswell, records the following exchange, which bears upon the subject of this book:

I told Goethe that I had lately been reading Winckelmann's
work upon the imitation of Greek works of art, and I confessed
it often seemed to me Winckelmann was not perfectly clear
about his subject.
"You are right," said Goethe, "we sometimes find him merely
groping about; but, what is the great matter, his groping always
leads to something. He is like Columbus, when he had not yet
discovered the New World, yet had a presentiment of it in his
mind. We learn nothing by reading him, but we become something. Now, Meyer has gone further, carried the knowledge of
art to its highest point. His history of art is an immortal work;
but he would not have become what he is, if, in his youth, he
had not formed himself on Winckelmann, and walked in the
path Winckelmann pointed out. You see once again what is done
for a man by a great predecessor, and the advantage of making
a proper use of him." (Eckermann 1836, 173)

The "immortal" work of Goethe's friend Johann Heinrich Meyer
and the man himself have faded from history and from art history

(unlike Winckelmann); but this does not affect the moral Goethe draws.

Goethe would have been the Great Writer to a literate speaker of German in the nineteenth and twentieth centuries (as Dante is to the Italians, Shakespeare to the English, Cervantes to the Spanish). Indeed, Goethe would also figure as the Great Man to those looking for a German culture hero, since his breadth of talents (as lyric and dramatic poet, scientist, statesman,[1] linguist, and translator) evoked Renaissance man from more than one commentator.[2]

We know from Freud's writings that he was greatly influenced by Goethe. He repeatedly quotes Goethe, using some quotations over and over again. (Strachey, in the Index volume of *The Complete Psychological Works of Sigmund Freud*, cites 142 references to Goethe and 45 to *Faust*.) Papini, in his less-than-reliable report of an interview with Freud, quotes him as saying, "Ever since childhood, my secret hero has been Goethe" (quoted by Yerushalmi 1989, 386). Freud was very much aware of Goethe as a scientist. Goethe published papers on anatomy, physics, botany, and zoology. He had a lifelong interest in studying animals and plants and did research in biological morphology; he developed and published an original (and wrong) theory of color; he was fascinated (like Freud) by archeology. Goethe both expressed and influenced the Zeitgeist of the nineteenth century. Consider the resonance Freud would have felt with such aphorisms of Goethe as

Animals, we have been told, are taught by their organs. But I would add, so are men, but men have this further advantage that they can also teach their organs in return. (Quoted in Auden and Kronenberger 1962, 6)

Freud, in his *Autobiography* (1925), attributes his decision to study medicine to Goethe's influence: "It was hearing Goethe's beautiful essay on Nature read aloud at a popular lecture by Professor Carl

1. "Through the fifty-eight years of his residence [in Weimar, Goethe's] duties and functions were to be amazingly varied. Essentially he was Prime Minister of the government, personal advisor to the Duke. In addition he was, at different times, overseer of natural resources, director of scientific and art institutions, Rector [president] of the University of Jena, supervisor of military recruitment; for long years he was director of the ducal theater. . . . [He] was entrusted with supervision of court festivities, especially when royalty visited from abroad. . . . He was, in short, foremost citizen in a sizable sector of the 'great world'" (Passage 1965, lvi).

2. "[Goethe] can be compared in versatility to Leonardo da Vinci, the Renais-

Bruhl just before I left school that decided me to become a medical student" (8).[3] Goethe's masterpiece is invoked when Freud adds that in his medical studies he "learned the truth of Mephistopheles' warning to Faust: 'It is in vain that you range from science to science: each man learns only what he can learn'" (9).

Freud specifically wrote at length of Goethe in two papers. In "A Childhood Recollection from *Dichtung und Wahrheit*" (1917), Freud attributes Goethe's memory of ostentatiously throwing crockery out of a window at age four to a symbolic expression of the firstborn son's hatred toward usurping younger siblings. He points to Goethe as an example of the advantage of being the mother's unrivaled favorite. (For Freud these were autobiographical themes.)

In 1930, Freud won the Goethe Prize of the city of Frankfurt. This was the only public award presented to Freud in his lifetime. It was, as the citation read, to be awarded to "a personality of established achievement whose creative work is worthy of an honour dedicated to Goethe's memory" (Freud 1930b, 206).[4] The recipient was supposed to respond in an address that illustrated his relationship to Goethe. Freud was too ill to speak before an audience, and his paper was read by Anna Freud at Goethe House in Frankfurt on August 28, 1930. To Dr. Alfons Paquet, who represented the prize committee, Freud wrote of the award (using the metaphor of burning that so often in his writings conveys both Freud's forbidden sexuality and his transcendent creativity and insight [see Shengold 1991]), "There is something about it that especially fires the imagination." He added that he was going to furnish "a few sentences . . . which deal with Goethe's connection with psycho-analysis and defending the analysts themselves against the reproaches of having offended against the respect due to the great man by the analytic attempts which have been made on him." This was Freud's adaptation of the theme proposed to him, of—as Freud put it—his "inner relation as a man and a scientist to Goethe" (207).

In his address, Freud briefly described how Goethe anticipated

---

sance Master, who like him was both artist and scientific investigator" (Freud 1930, 208).

3. Actually the essay was not by Goethe but by a Swiss writer, G. C. Tobler; as an old man Goethe apparently found it in a pile of his papers and mistakenly included it among his own works.

4. See Yerushalmi's [1989] convincing and fascinating refutation of the popular assumption that the prize was awarded primarily for literature.

psychoanalytic findings. He quoted from the opening lines of Goethe's dedication to *Faust,* which describe the power over the mind of "erste Lieb' und Freundschaft" (first love and friendship). To Freud this illustrated Goethe's intuitive assumption of what we call the genetic hypothesis of psychoanalysis, the force engendered to our motivations by "those first inclinations [that] take figures from one's own family circle as their object" (209).[5] (Freud is alluding both to the Oedipus complex—the theme over which Freud was later to quarrel with Goethe's supposed grandson, Jung [see below]—and to Family Romance fantasies.)

Freud next adduced Goethe's interest in dreams.[6] He described an attempt Goethe made to perform a kind of psychotherapy on a woman whom he directed to do the equivalent of free association: to say everything that came into her mind.

Freud then repeated the remark (first expressed in his paper on Dostoyevsky [1928]) that psychoanalysis was inadequate to solve the mysteries of artistic creativity. He ended the short address with an apology for not having succeeded very far in understanding Goethe—an explanation pertinent to someone trying to understand Freud himself. Freud used a quotation he often applied to his own remarks:

> This is because Goethe was not only, as a poet, a great self-revealer, but also, in spite of the abundance of autobiographical records, a careful concealer. We cannot help thinking here of the words of Mephistopheles: "The best of what you know may not, after all, be told to boys" (*Faust* Part I Scene 4) (212).

Freud felt an obvious identification with Goethe in that both were the firstborn sons of very young mothers. Goethe's mother was eighteen when he was born; his father was forty. Sigmund's mother was twenty, his father forty-one. The identification becomes

5. Goethe was in many ways realistic about sexual matters. Eckermann, in a discussion with Goethe about a commentary on Sophocles' *Antigone*, quotes the commentator as making the "assertion that family piety appears most pure in woman, and especially a sister; and that a sister can love only a brother with perfect purity and without sexual feeling. . . . [Goethe responds], 'As if we did not know of numerous cases where the most sensual inclinations have existed between brother and sister, both knowingly and unknowingly'" (Eckermann 1836, 177). This comes close to being a "Freudian" assumption of unconscious incestuous wishes.

6. Kurt Eissler in his encyclopaedic study of Goethe (1963) points out that Goethe, like Freud, had an identification with the biblical Joseph (see 1102–04).

manifest to the reader of Freud's paper on Goethe's "childhood recollection." Goethe had a sister, Cornelia, born when he was fifteen months old. She was the only other survivor of "a considerable family of very weakly children" (1917, 150). It is Freud's (to me dubious) thesis that the scant differences in the ages of the children spared Goethe from jealousy of Cornelia,[7] who was a favorite of the poet's as long as she lived—into her midtwenties—and one of the deepest emotional attachments of Goethe's life. Certainly Cornelia's being a fellow survivor helped preserve the positive part of Goethe's ambivalence. There were four other siblings born subsequently who died before Goethe was twelve. By the time he was four (his age at the breaking of the crockery), two other "disturbing intruders" (Freud 1917, 152) had been born: Herrmann Jakob, born when Johann was three, died at the age of six, when Johann was ten; and Katherina, born when he was five, died when Goethe was six.

Freud's brother Julius was born when Sigmund was eleven months old. Freud's sister Anna was born when he was two and a half. Four more girls and another brother were born by the time Sigmund was ten. This was an even more "considerable" family than Goethe's (and they survived). The repeated threat of these births to the spoiled firstborn darling would have been part of Freud's empathic understanding of Goethe's exhibitionistic act of tossing out of the window the crockery newly bought by his mother as a "violent expression [of the] wish of getting rid of a disturbing intruder [Herrmann Jakob]" (1917, 152).

Freud does not specifically mention it here, but of course the more primal (and the more needed) "disturbing intruder" is the father (Freud's Jacob, who could have been evoked by "Herrman Jakob"), whose centrality to the mother is a greater threat and to

7. Perhaps Freud's statement has something to do with the great significance his brother Julius, born when Freud was only eleven months old, had for him. One would expect intense sibling hatred, and this was undoubtedly present because Freud attests to it in his description of his guilt of the survivor when his brother died at eight months of age. I would assume that there was much reaction formation (love emphasized to distance the threatening intensity of hate) in Goethe's great fondness for Cornelia. Freud also says, in his explanation of the sparing of Cornelia, that children generally turn most of the hostility away from existing siblings to the newcomers. This is convincing since the diversion of the mother toward another would be repeated, but obviously there is room for all sorts of individual variations on the endlessly variable themes of sibling rivalries and affections.

whose superior sexual equipment and powers the child dimly attributes responsibility for the creation of the intruding siblings.
Sibling rivalry, powerfully motivated in its own right as competition
for the exclusive attention of a parent (or both parents), is also and
chiefly a displacement of oedipal rivalry with a parent. The indispensable parent is preserved, the dispensable sibling gets the murderous wishes in concentrated form. Thus the first murder is that
of Abel by Cain.

Being a military hero, a conquistador, was the subject of Freud's
early daydreams. He certainly could have written of himself, as he
does of Goethe,

> If a man has been his mother's undisputed darling, he retains
> throughout life the triumphant feeling ["jenes erobererge-
> fuhl"—literally, "those feelings of a conqueror"][8], the confidence
> in success which not seldom brings actual success along with it.
> (156)

Freud's mother, Amalie, who even when he was a famous professor called her darling firstborn "mein Goldener Sigi," is described by Jones (1953) as possessing "gaiety, alertness and sharp-
witted intelligence" (3). These are also attributes of Goethe's
mother. Neither mother was intellectual but had a coarse, earthy,
humorous toughness. They were somebodies and commanded respect. Freud ends the conqueror remark quoted above with,
"Goethe might well have given some such heading to his autobiography as: 'My strength has its roots in my relation to my mother'"
(156). And so might well have Freud.

Goethe as a grown man stayed away from his mother, who was
always boasting about her famous pride and joy. Freud kept his
widowed mother in his household. But in his emotional life, theories, and thinking he too needed to distance her. The Oedipus
complex was first described as the father complex; and Freud
needed prompting by his female followers and analysands before
he could begin to pay due attention to the primary importance of
the mother, mothering, and the whole preoedipal period of devel-

8. Freud, in a letter to Fliess (February 1, 1900), writes this disclaimer: "For I
am actually not at all a man of science, not an observer, not an experimenter, not
a thinker. I am by temperament nothing but a conquistador—an adventurer, if you
want it translated—with all the curiosity, daring, and tenacity characteristic of a man
of this sort" (1985, 398).

opment. This avoidance was especially prevalent during his early years of psychoanalytic writing in relation to hostile wishes of the son toward the mother and the impact of the threat of losing her. When Jacob Freud died in 1896, the forty-one-year-old Sigmund described a father's death as "the most important event, the most poignant loss, in a man's life" (1900b, xxvi). He still had his mother and with this generalization seems to have been obviously distancing the possibility of losing her. Freud, after the death of Eitingon's mother in 1929, wrote to console his friend, "The loss of a mother must be something very strange, not comparable with anything else and it must arouse emotions which are difficult to grasp. For I have a mother of my own and she bars my way to the desired rest, the eternal Nothing; I could not, so to speak, forgive myself were I to die before her" (1992, 49). Both Freud and Goethe had intense ambivalent feelings toward their adoring mothers.

Freud, like so many other German-speaking intellectuals, felt himself to be a spiritual descendant of Goethe. A much younger psychoanalytic German-speaker, Carl Jung, had, as part of his Family Romance fantasies, the vague legend that his paternal grandfather, also called Carl Gustav Jung, was an illegitimate son of Goethe. He communicated this to Freud early in their acquaintance. Jung's biographer writes,

> The grandson was so much taken with the legend of this illustrious illegitimacy that in his head it became a quasi-certainty. Goethe was, to him, the highest embodiment of creativity, [Goethe's] Faust the modern counterpart to Oedipus. In letters and talks with friends, Jung often alluded to *the* great-grandfather as if his blood tie to Goethe were a proven fact. And if, on occasion, he felt called upon to repudiate the legend of his descent as "annoying," he usually did so in a tone that denied his denial. (Stern 1976, 18–19)[9]

Goethe nourished both Freud's and Jung's fantasies and influenced their ideals. They were specifically steeped in *Faust,* and their works abound in quotations from that great work and other references

9. Jung, in his autobiography (1961), writes, "The story goes that Sophie Ziegler (the wife of my great-grandfather [Franz Ignaz Jung, d. 1832]) had an illegitimate child by Goethe, and that this child was my grandfather, Carl Gustav Jung. This was considered virtually an established fact. My grandfather says not a word about it in his diaries, however" (35). Jung's editor, Aniela Jaffe, adds, "No proof of this

to Goethe. (These are spectacularly present in their mutual correspondence.)

When he was sixteen, Jung's mother suggested to him that he
read *Faust.* Jung (1961) writes,

> It poured into my soul like a miraculous balm. "Here at last,"
> I thought, "is someone who takes the devil seriously and even
> concludes a blood pact with him.". . . Faust was plainly a bit of
> a windbag. I had the impression that the weight of the drama
> and its significance lay chiefly on the side of Mephistopheles. . . .
> The real problem, it seemed to me, lay with Mephistopheles,
> whose whole figure made the deepest impression on me, and
> who, I vaguely sensed, had a relationship to the mystery of the
> Mothers. At any rate Mephistopheles and the great initiation at
> the end remained for me a wonderful and mysterious experi-
> ence on the fringes of my conscious world. (1961, 60)

Jung's father was a parson, and in Carl's boyhood and early
adolescence he passionately obsessed about the devil and God, who
were featured in his dreams and fantasies. Jung, like Freud, associated Goethe with his decision to study medicine (see 1961, 86).
Carl's struggles with his father took place largely in relation to
religious discussions. About his late teens, the old Jung writes,

> *Faust,* as I [then] realized with something of a shock, meant
> more to me than my beloved Gospel according to St. John.
> There was something in *Faust* that worked directly on my feel-
> ings. John's Christ was strange to me. (1961, 87)

In the correspondence between Freud and Jung, Goethe usually
plays the role of the good one, the devil the role of the bad one.
But, as Jung shows in relation to Mephistopheles, with whom he
identified, there is much ambivalence about both figures. Faust
himself sometimes stands with and sometimes against Mephistoph-

---

item of family tradition has been found in the available sources, the archives of the
Goethehaus in Frankfurt am Main and the baptismal register in the Jesuitenkirche
in Mannheim. Goethe was not in Mannheim at the period in question, and there is
no record of Sophie Ziegler's staying in Weimar or anywhere in Goethe's vicinity.
Jung used to speak of this stubbornly persistent legend with a certain gratified
amusement, for it might serve to explain one subtle aspect of his fascination with
Goethe's *Faust;* it belonged to an inner reality as it were. . . . On the other hand he
would also call the story 'annoying'" (35–36).

eles, who can be viewed as an externalized—projected—part of himself.

When Jung, as an old man, was asked about publishing his correspondence with Freud, he said that he felt the letters were not of great scientific interest. In the sense that they contain no new exposition of thought, he was right. There is important dialogue about psychosis and narcissism (areas that are still being explored and defined). And the reader gets a sense of the two men learning from each other and of the development of their ideas. Jung had the access to hospitalized schizophrenics that Freud lacked in 1907, when their acquaintance began. It was from Jung that Freud derived the supposed "*fact* that these patients reveal their complexes without resistance and are inaccessible to transference" (35; my italics)—a too-simple and mistaken notion that Freud used as a basis for some of his theorizing. In the years of contact with Jung, his letters to the younger man show Freud at work on several of his basic concepts. But there is not the same active exchange of ideas or as much opportunity to see Freud working out his thought as in Freud's letters to Fliess.

Both sets of letters permit study of the relationship between scientific ideas and the complexes (Jung's term for unconscious clusters of ideas and feelings) that, as Freud had discovered, determined them. We see what the two men meant to each other and how their major relationships were mutually invoked. The themes of rivalry with father and with brothers and of homosexual love predominate in the Freud/Jung correspondence. For Freud, all his revenants come to life in relation to Jung: father, older brother, younger brother, mother, sister, early playmate, and, above all, Wilhelm Fliess, "the arch-revenant" (Schur 1972). We have seen that the neurotic relationship to Fliess served as subject matter for Freud's self-analysis. As he had done before with Fliess, Freud relived his earliest years in relation to Jung, but with a difference. Jung came into his life after Freud had achieved his initial mastery of psychoanalysis and written *The Interpretation of Dreams* and after he had worked at his self-analysis with the resultant partial transcendence of his transference to Fliess. Jung was to attain *his* mastery only after the end of the relationship with Freud and the breakdown that followed it. We know less of Jung's early life than we do of Freud's, but in these letters we see his crucial relationships focus onto Freud: owing to Jung's "transference," which Freud in these letters describes as "the universal tendency to keep making new prints of the clichés we bear within us" (98).

Jones, who had read the men's correspondence in preparation for his biography of Freud, compares Freud's attachments to Fliess and to Jung, noting similarities but stating that Freud's feeling toward Jung was far less intense. This is obviously so, yet the intensity revealed by their letters is much greater than Jones leads his readers to expect. Indeed, one wonders if, as Jones implies, the greater attachment was always Jung's.[10] Clearly Jung was left with more involvement. Freud seems to have been able to contain and reduce his wishes toward his "son and heir" while Jung ended the relationship in a near-paranoid blaze of hatred that introduced a period of intense psychic pathology. But Freud found in Jung, as he had in Fliess, something he longed for—the prospect of magic, a narcissistic promise which corresponded to something Freud mistrusted in his own personality and felt as a deficiency that would be supplied by another man: "I have always felt that there is something about my personality, my ideas and manner of speaking, that people find strange and repellent, whereas all hearts are open to you" (Freud to Fliess, 1954, 82). It is important to recall that Jung entered Freud's life at a time when preoedipal and oedipal conflicts partly change their direction, and the father as unconscious rival and as sexual object is joined by the son—a son, too, can promise magical solutions.

There are many references in both men's letters to Jung as the grandchild of an illegitimate son of Goethe. To Freud, so conscious of his fifty-plus years (as the friendship begins), this supposed offspring of Goethe, his very name connoting youth,[11] suddenly appeared as Mephistopheles had to Faust, promising magic and

10. Cf. Trilling's opinion: "But if the admirers of Freud are troubled by discerning so much purpose in his relation to Jung, they are not likely to be reassured by those many passages in the letters which suggest that the courtship was not only professional and calculated but also personal and very deeply felt, much more so, indeed, that Freud permitted himself to know. No man is to be faulted for the love he gives or the love he seeks, yet moved as we may be by Freud's need for Jung's loyal affection, I think we have the right to ask of the father of psychoanalysis a little more consciousness of the nature and extent of the claims he makes on Jung than Freud here shows" (1974, 179).

11. *Jung* is the German word for "young": Freud to Jung, letter 23F: "Don't take the burden of representing me too hard. You are so enviably *young* and independent" (1974, 42).

beckoning the "old man" out of his comparatively provincial Viennese-Jewish microcosm toward the wide world of official scientific and intellectual acceptance. Like Fliess before him, Jung showed a great self-confidence and seemed surrounded by the aura of success. He promised the marvelous—his first publication was about the psychological implications of the occult, in which he had a lifelong interest and belief. (Freud had a leaning toward the occult himself, but it was usually accompanied by a healthy skepticism.) Under the influence of "the magic of [Jung's] personal presence" (218), Freud allowed himself temporarily and intermittently to share in Jung's belief. Jung had corresponding feelings toward Freud. He writes him in an early letter, "Anyone who knows your science has veritably eaten of the tree of paradise and become clairvoyant" (56). (Jung, the son of a minister, eventually assigns the roles of both God and the Devil to Freud.)

The figure of the devil or the demon (largely borrowed from Goethe's *Faust*) was a recurrent metaphor for Freud (see Kanzer 1961). Fliess had appeared to Freud in the Mephistophelean guise: "Demon," Freud addresses Fliess in 1895, "you Demon! Why don't you write to me? How are you? Don't you care at all anymore what I'm doing?" (Schur 1972, 87). Here Fliess is reproached for not answering a letter, as Freud was so often to reproach Jung. The devil is mentioned dozens of times in the Freud/Jung letters; he was called up by their relationship. In their letters, the devil is used as a metaphor for the instinctual, for the bad father, for the seducer (heterosexual or homosexual), and for the guide toward wisdom (like Mephistopheles), for the creative daemon of the unconscious, and for each other. The relationship between Freud and Jung during the years of their attachment can be seen as a love story, full of suppressed ambivalence and with a bad ending, a repetition of Freud's relationship with Fliess. One man transcends the homosexual impulses involved and learns from them; the other finds them too much for him, denies them, and breaks down (in what Freud calls "paranoia").[12]

Jung (like Karl Abraham, his rival "son and heir") was twenty

12. Freud writes to Jung in 1910 about the rebelling Alfred Adler: "In me he awakens the memory of Fliess, but an octave lower. The same paranoia" (376). He would eventually feel this in relation to Jung (see Donn 1988). Donn quotes a letter of 1910 from Freud to Ferenczi: "Adler is a little Fliess come to life again," and she convincingly sets the reappearance of Fliess in relation to Adler as also pertaining to Freud's homosexual feelings toward Jung.

years younger than Freud. As I have noted, this was a meaningful age difference for Freud, whose twenty-year-older half-brother, Phillip, was a bad father figure for him as a child. In one letter, Freud assumes the role of Philip of Macedon, calling Jung "dear son Alexander" (300), Freud's younger brother's name, and declaring to his appointed successor (whom he is reassuring about "resistances that arise from your [Jung's] father complex") that he has left him much to conquer. The correspondence starts with a Moses-like invocation of a successor (Freud later calls Jung his Joshua [196]) in which the motif of age addressing youth is first sounded: "In view of my age (50), I hardly expect to see the end of the struggle, but my follower will I hope" (6). Here was a new edition of Fliess in the figure of a son who would be the repeatedly sought-for other, the one elect person who, like Fliess before him, would appreciate Freud and help fulfill his destiny.[13] Jung, for his part, was looking for a father. His minister father, the man in black who haunts his autobiography, had died in 1899. He and Freud quickly took to each other and cemented a master-disciple relationship so that after several months of correspondence Jung talked of colleagues moving "closer to *our* side" (9; my italics).

In the early letters, partly in relation to a kind of confessional on Jung's part (a recurrent form of communication for him), conflicted and unpleasant aspects of Jung's character are revealed. He displays ambivalence toward authority, a need both to defy and to submit. He reveals a tendency to sacrifice truth to court acceptance: "As you rightly say, I leave our opponents a line of retreat, with the conscious purpose of not making recantation too difficult for them. . . . If I appear to underestimate the therapeutic results of psychoanalysis, I do so only out of *diplomatic* considerations" (10–11; my italics). Freud, to whom equivocation and diplomacy were so alien, plays the role of analyst, gently and tolerantly underlining Jung's failings. Jung is alternately apologetic and righteous, often writing in terms that seem to express blunt honesty: "I speak of things as I understand them and as I believe is right" (15). Freud feels inclined to see the diplomacy as practical know-how. Here was another man with those qualities of assurance and practicality that Freud felt he lacked.[14] And surely this man who so

13. Freud seems not to have sought a successor from among his own sons; his daughter Anna was to play this role.

14. For example, Freud writes to Fliess, "I read through your draft in a single

inspired him with confidence could never be a confidence man. Freud expected that his influence would banish Jung's waverings and his need for a diplomat's psychology. Jung, after all, had spontaneously agreed to Freud's request "to trust me for the present in matters where your experience does not yet enable you to make up your own mind. . . . I believe I deserve such trust" (13).

But Freud was still Freud enough to see the danger of character defect; he writes Jung that "in our special circumstances, the utmost frankness is the best diplomacy" (18). In retrospect, Jung's reply to this seems significant: "I am still young [*noch Jung*], and now and then *one* has *one's* quirks in the matter of recognition and scientific standing" (20; my italics emphasize the shift from the first to the third person, which seems to me to compromise Jung's "I" and evade responsibility). Jung follows this with, "I shall never abandon any portion of your theory *that is essential to me*" (20; my italics). Here the confidence man seems to be speaking. Robert Fliess once told me that when he met Freud in the 1930s, he asked for the old man's opinion of Jung. Fliess said he would never forget how Freud grimaced in disgust and muttered, "Bad character!" Right or wrong, such a judgment was far from Freud's feeling in 1907.

Freud himself does not emerge from these letters with his character unscathed. For example, there is something apologetic and repellent, something perhaps reminiscent of Freud's father stepping aside into the gutter to let the Christian pass, in Freud's repeated awareness of how valuable the adherence of the Christian Jung will be for the spread of psychoanalysis, which had been so closely associated with Jews. Trilling remarked, "It isn't likely that the admirers of either man will be gratified by the part he plays in the correspondence. Freud and Jung were not good for one another; their connection made them susceptible to false attitudes and ambiguous tones" (1974, 178).

After their first meeting in Vienna, Jung wrote Freud rapturously of "the tremendous impression you have made on me. . . . I hope my work for your cause will show you the depths of my

---

breath. I liked tremendously its easy assurance, the natural, almost self-evident way in which each point leads to the next, its unpretentious unfolding of riches" (Freud 1954, 42). The draft mentioned was about the relationships between the nose and sex, and this letter shows the infatuated Freud's credulity (see Jones 1953). Jung, during the first years following 1907, was evoking a reprise of Freud's infatuation with and waiver of judgment toward Fliess.

gratitude and veneration. I hope and even dream that we may welcome you in Zurich. . . . A visit from you would be seventh heaven for me personally" (26).

Freud replied that Jung had "inspired me with confidence for the future. . . . I now realize that I am as replaceable as everyone else and that I could hope for no one better than yourself, as I have come to know you, to continue and complete my work" (27). This is from a letter of April 7, 1907, written shortly after the first meeting between the two men in early March. Freud seems to have found his replacement as psychoanalytic leader with an astonishing speed that smacks of impatience—again, the "cannibalistic affect." He does not appear to have been aware that in choosing his successor he was stirring up what Schur (1972) calls the guilt of the survivor, which began with Freud's reaction to the death of his younger brother Julius—one of the two people from his childhood (Freud had written to another Julius revenant, the slightly younger Fliess) who "now determine the neurotic element, but also the intensity of all my friendships" (1954, 219).

Jung reacts to the first meeting like a new analysand who has transferred positive feelings onto his analyst and has for the time being acquired conviction: "The last shreds of doubt . . . about the rightness of your theory . . . were dispelled by my stay in Vienna" (26). But his underlying ambivalence quickly shows. Freud proposes sending Jung a patient he has seen—the "boy from Gorlitz" (35), who is "a highly gifted individual, an Oedipus type, loves his mother, hates his father. . . . He is the first case we shall both have been able to observe directly" (33). Freud adds many details about the boy's sexual fantasies and behavior. Jung uneasily replies (to this proffered mutuality as well as to the prospect of living evidence of Freud's sexual and, specifically, oedipal theories) that there is no room for the boy at the clinic "at present" (35), but he also includes in his letter observations about sexual disturbances in schizophrenics. Freud then sends him a theoretical dissertation on paranoia which includes his well-known saying that "anyone who gives more than he has is a rogue" (40). Freud learns from Jung about the "lack of resistance and the fragility of transference" (42) in dementia praecox and shares with him his concept of the psychosis as a regression to autoerotism. Freud is expressing ideas and concepts that he had first written about to Fliess in the 1890s (for example, the use of projection in paranoia). Freud closes by suggesting,

"Perhaps you will be able to take on the boy from Gorlitz later. His case ought to be most instructive" (42).

Jung does not reply for a while; he says the "long pause" is somehow due to Freud's remarks on paranoia, but one wonders whether it is not also evoked by the "boy from Gorlitz," who had become, I speculate, a talisman for Jung that threatened to evoke frightening anal, homosexual, and negative oedipal wishes.[15] The closeness seems to be telling on Jung. He has trouble understanding Freud's thinking about the linkage of homosexual feeling and paranoia. Jung makes an analogy to dementia praecox patients which those who have read about his childhood religious obsessive struggles can see applies to himself:

> The following analogy has always struck me as enlightening; the religious ecstatic who longs for God is one day vouchsafed a vision of God. But the conflict with reality also creates the opposite for him: certainty turns into doubt, God into the devil, and the sublimated sexual joy of the *unio mystica* into sexual anxiety with all its historical spectres. (44)

In response to Jung's "pauses" in replying, Freud begins to crave Jung's letters with impatience; he reproaches him for his delays (46). A later statement of this seems almost to convey (as an illustration of the thesis of this book) that Jung has become part of Freud's mental self: "My personality was impoverished by the interruption of our correspondence" (76). Jung brings to Freud, as Fliess had done, the promise of future fulfillment—the son will make the father immortal. Jung's fulsome praise, expressed in oral body language—"Your *Gravida* is magnificent, I gulped it at one go" (49)—is responded to by Freud with, "To tell the truth, a statement such as yours means more to me than the approval of a whole medical congress; for one thing it makes the approval of future congresses *a certainty*" (52; my italics). And Jung replies in ecstatic metaphors of anal and oral contact: "I rejoice every day in your riches and live from the crumbs that fall from the rich man's table" (56).

15. In the same letter, Jung writes, "Your Gorlitz patient now has unquestionably catatonic symptoms on the lowest autoerotic level—he's started smearing himself. So his father wrote me recently. Any psychic treatment, even mere [*sic*] analysis, is completely out of the question, as unfortunately I see everyday with my own catatonics" (45).

As their mutual positive feelings intensify, the concomitant hostility is directed onto their opponents. Freud sends Jung "two bombshells from the enemy camp" (53). Jung is a master of vituperation: "These pachyderms just can't understand anything unless you write it out as big as your fist on their hides" (49).[16] Freud at times reflects Jung's coarseness, and the two gleefully continue to vilify their enemies until enmity breaks out between them.

In the summer of 1907, a new figure appears in the correspondence, one who was to bring triangular complications to the sublimated homosexual romance: Karl Abraham. Jung confesses that he is "jealous" (78) of Freud's interest in Abraham (whom Freud had not yet met but with whom he had exchanged a few letters) and tries to master his hostility toward him. Abraham distrusts Jung, having been with him at Burghölzli since 1904, but Freud will not listen to Abraham's warnings. Jung criticizes Abraham, attributing to him character traits of his own—"highly adaptable"— and declaring that Abraham is "totally lacking in psychological empathy, for which reason he is usually very unpopular with the patients" (78). But Jung admits his bias. Freud is interested in Abraham's name and whether he is Jewish: "Is he a descendant of his eponym?" Jung replies that Abraham "is what his name implies" (81). (We have seen that Abraham's name is far from an incidental factor here.) In a letter in which he apologizes for a three-week break in the correspondence, Jung cites as an excuse that his duties at Burghölzli were heavier than usual because "Professor Bleuler and the 1st assistant went on holiday" (76). "The 1st assistant" was Abraham, who had recently been promoted—Bleuler may not have shared Jung's views about Abraham's difficulty with "psychological empathy"—and who had been mentioned before by name in the correspondence. "Father Abraham" Jung was already expressing his conflict with Karl Abraham by erasing Abraham's *name* (see chapter 6).

In September of 1907 Jung sends what sounds like a lover's

16. Stern: "These diatribes against colleagues escalated quickly. In strident tones Jung spoke of 'psychopaths' and of 'pachyderms'. . . ; he hurled epithets such as 'vain old duffer,' 'totally impotent gasbag,' 'confounded fusspot,' 'incredibly plebeian,' 'miserable pen-pusher,' 'damned swine,' 'complete nut,' 'slimy bastard,' etc. Freud, more subdued, could not quite keep up with this flood of invective, but his letters, too, teemed with 'hidings' and 'whippings' he wanted to administer to unbelievers" (1976, 83). The pupil was leading the master here—Jung becoming a transient ego ideal.

request for a "photograph of you, not as you used to look but as you did when I first got to know you." Jung wants it "dearly. . . . I would be ever so grateful because again and again I feel the want of your picture" (86). The men exchange pictures, which seems "almost absurd" to Jung: the honeymoon is at its height. Jung inveighs in his coarse fashion against Eitingon and Gross for their supposed sexual immorality; he is feeling the pressure of his own homosexual libido with its "undeniable erotic undertone" (95).

The following month, a year and a half after the correspondence began, there is a confessional letter from Jung which shows considerable personal analytic insight and, in retrospect, seems to have provided a watershed in the two men's relationship. In it Jung commits a slip of the pen on the word "honestly" (*redlich*), which he attributes to an "evil spirit that . . . bedevils my pen." His "boundless admiration" for Freud has the nature of a "'religious' crush . . . though it does not really bother me, I still feel it as disgusting and ridiculous because of its *undeniable erotic undertone*. This abominable feeling comes from the fact that as a boy I was the victim of a sexual assault by a man I once worshipped" (95; my italics).

Jung adds that this hampers him: "I find psychological insight makes relations with colleagues who have a strong sexual transference to me downright disgusting.[17] *I therefore fear your confidence*. I also fear the same reaction from you when I speak of my intimate affairs" (95).

Jung's confession showed that he had actually lived out the requirements of Freud's early theory of neurosogenesis—he had been seduced as a child by a father figure. In making his own confidence to Freud, Jung was in the position of an analysand starting to acknowledge his full awareness of a transference—insight so charged with unpredictable dynamism that it could ulti-

17. Jung may have continued to have troubles, not only with male colleagues, but also with male patients. Stern says that "Jung's clientele was recruited largely from two, partly overlapping, categories: Anglo-Saxons and women." He continues, "Jung's magnetism for female neurotics of all shades was remarkable; it became irresistible if such women happened to be British or American. Part of Jung's secret was that he empathized strongly with the aspirations of women who were or felt misunderstood; undoubtedly his extreme, almost 'feminine' sensitivity also contributed to this peculiar sex-appeal. In any case, women were his first, most enthusiastic, and most fanatic disciples. In Zurich medical circles, these overly rapturous devotees were tagged with the inevitable label 'Jung-Frauen'" (Stern 1976, 63).

mately liberate him or at least ameliorate his involvement and potentially increase the feelings of closeness that inevitably touched off his disgust and hostility. The "man [he] once worshipped," whoever he was (a friend of Jung's father according to Donn [1988, 49]), must at least have had the significance for the sexually assaulted boy of his pastor father and of the Christian God with whom Jung was so ambivalently obsessed in his youth. (He had a repetitive fantasy associating God with a giant turd.)

At first the confession seemed to clear the air. Freud had good expectations and drew closer to the Jung who was struggling painfully to be honest, changing the salutation of his letters from "Lieber College" (Dear Colleague) to "Lieber Freund und College" (Dear Friend and Colleague]:

> What you say of your inner development sounds reassuring; a transference on a religious basis would strike me as most disastrous. It could only end in apostasy. (98)

Here the future of the relationship is outlined. Unfortunately, the confession seems to have been followed by its suppression, not by a working through. The story is never referred to again in the correspondence, and it does not appear in Jung's autobiography. Jung continues to fear and court a reenactment, and the predominantly suppressed resistance to this is to burst out years later.

Freud had begun to see with increasing clarity the links between paranoia and homosexuality:[18] in patients, in the Schreber *Memoirs* he was to read at Jung's suggestion, and in his thoughts about his relationship with Fliess (whom he again designates as paranoid). But Freud does not see the danger in his relationship—despite Jung's warning—with the younger man who had been seduced as a child, toward whom he expresses his affection (and underlying erotic wishes) as toward a son in praising a lecture of Jung: "Spirit of my spirit, I can say with pride, but at the same time, something artistic and soft, lofty and serene, something ingratiating that I could never have produced" (115). This sentiment seems bound to provoke Jung's disgust, and it is hardly surprising that Jung did not reply for several weeks. This sort of interruption punctuates the correspondence, with Jung providing an astonishing variety of

---

18. I think today we would modify the linkage (making it less general) to that between paranoia and a destructive, murderous, primitive homosexuality. This is an area that still needs much exploration.

excuses in relation to Freud's reproachful impatience. Keeping the fretful, overeager Freud waiting involved a kind of sadomasochistic teasing.[19]

Jung writes that he wants to establish a relationship different from the one between Freud and Fliess: "Let me enjoy your friendship not as one between equals but as that of father and son. . . . This distance [*sic*] appears to me only fitting and natural" (122). This letter, written only four months after Jung's confession, shows no awareness that oedipal feelings between "unequals" imply the opposite of "distance," feelings that for Jung involved a combination of parricidal and homosexual wishes that could lead to (Fliess-like, as Freud and Jung viewed it) paranoia. (One feels— like Trilling—that both men should have known better.) Jung ends his letter in language that suggests unconscious pregnancy fantasies: "Your views on paranoia have not *lain fallow*" (122; my italics).

Jung then becomes overinvolved with a kind of equal. The brilliant, erratic psychiatrist Otto Gross had lost his colleague status when he was certified into Burghölzli for drug addiction. Like the would-be mutual patient, the "boy from Gorlitz," Gross had previously consulted Freud. Shortly after Gross was hospitalized, Jung writes Freud that he had completed Gross's analysis (in two weeks!); he had been working intensively with him and had been analyzing Gross's homosexuality. At first Jung did not see that Gross was what he was later to call psychotic: "I have let everything drop and have spent all my available time, *day and night,* pushing on with his analysis. . . . Whenever I got stuck, he analyzed me" (156; my italics). There was certainly a narcissistic mirroring confrontation between Jung and Gross, and reversible roles (paralleling those of Freud and Jung) were enacted by their mutual analysis. Perhaps the intensity of Jung's involvement ("day and night") can be explained by the opportunity Gross provided for reversing from passive to active the role Jung had predominantly played with Freud, in which his own homosexuality was being revived and, potentially, "analyzed." But Gross could not stand the heat of this

19. In 1910, Jung writes, again evoking the devil, "I am in good shape and still have resistances to writing you at the right time, my conscious motivation being that I must select a particularly undisturbed moment which of course never comes until one takes it. The reason for the resistance is my father-complex, my inability to come up to expectations (one's own work is garbage, says the devil)" (297).

reversible father/son confrontation and ran away from the hospital.[20] *Then* Jung recognized his patient's psychosis[21] and something of his own (counter)identification with the fascinating and intelligent Gross: "He often seemed like my twin brother" (156). But brother Jung had gotten too close by pushing to be father or son. Freud flatly characterizes Gross as paranoid in a letter whose concluding "by the way" sentence was not calculated to discourage Jung's fear of passive homosexual strivings: "In conclusion, a little peculiar item; I recently came across your birthday in a medical dictionary: 26 June . . . it's my wife's birthday" (160).

In the spring of 1909, there was a marked infusion of the familiar devil motif into the correspondence. Freud was anxious over yet another gap in communication (these hiatuses evoked not only Fliess but, as unconscious symbols, the female genitals). Jung had delayed this time because again he had something to confess— a serious countertransference involvement with a female patient at Burghölzli who was also a colleague. This was Sabina Spielrein, who was to become a talented psychoanalyst, and whose at least emotional seduction by Jung has become well known through the book by Carotenuto (1980). Jung fell in love with the intelligent young Russian-Jewish girl after he had helped her emerge from a psychoticlike withdrawal (Jung's diagnosis was "hysterical psychosis"). The relationship, part therapeutic and part personal, continued for some years after Spielrein left the hospital; during this time she undertook medical training (at Jung's suggestion) in order eventu-

20. Jung was to repeat the relationship with Gross when he took on as disciple, acted as psychiatrist/adviser to, and interfered with the life of a younger colleague, Johann Honegger. Here too a kind of mutual "analysis" took place. Honegger killed himself in 1911 after breaking with his fiancée on Jung's advice. Gross too ended as a suicide.

21. I do not mean to suggest that we can accept Jung's (and Freud's) diagnosis of the complicated Gross, who appears to have been drug-addicted, psychopathic, narcissistic, but also handsome, charming, brilliant, tormented. His career is fascinating. He was seen by Freud as an original thinker, but an untrustworthy and perhaps even dangerous one. Gross believed in a kind of unrestrained eroticism and was a drug addict for a good part of his life. He had been the lover of two of the beautiful and intelligent von Richthofen sisters, who both influenced and were influenced by him: Else, whom he seduced when she was married to a man named Jaffe and who went on to marry the great sociologist Max Weber; and the even more famous Frieda, married to the philologist Ernest Weekley at the time of the affair but whose second husband and lifelong preoccupation was D. H. Lawrence (see Green 1974).

ally to become a psychiatrist. She was already in love with him, and Jung encouraged this when he began to respond emotionally. Sabina wanted to have his child and spoke to others about her love for her doctor/mentor.[22] This frightened Jung. Carotenuto describes:

> An anonymous letter, which Sabina suspects was written by Jung's wife, informs Sabina's parents of the situation. They demand an explanation from Jung and the answer promptly arrives, a letter that is a genuine *coup de théâtre,* a sensational and unexpected change of mask. Jung writes to Sabina's mother that he is not there to gratify her daughter's sensuality and that he wishes to be free of her and her demands. (1982, 176)

In response to Sabina's mother's reproach to him for encouraging such emotional closeness, Jung replies in this coarse and nasty letter (see Freud/Jung, 236), in effect: if you don't like my falling in love with your daughter, why don't you pay me my private fee for our sessions? The letter shows a good deal of Jung's "bad character," and he had enough decency to be ashamed of having written it. Jung turned to Freud for confession and comfort: "It was a piece of knavery which I very reluctantly confess to you *as my father*" (236; my italics).

It is not known how much sexual contact took place between Jung and Spielrein. According to her diary, "several times we sat 'in tender embrace,'" and she tells of "single moments, when I rested in his arms" (Carotenuto 1980, 11, 12). Later in the diary

---

22. It is fascinating that Spielrein wanted to call this child Siegfried, the name Wagner gave in *The Ring* to the son of Siegmund! Freud's disgruntled Viennese colleagues and disciples who were jealous of Freud's paternal attitude were wont to call Jung the blond Siegfried. Spielrein was very much aware of the triangle between Freud, Jung, and herself, and she expressed jealousy of Jung's love for Freud. There was also for her a triangle with Jung and his wife, apparently encouraged by Jung. Spielrein writes, "When he gave me his diary to read, he said in a very soft, hoarse voice, 'Only my wife has read this . . . and you.' He said no one could understand him as I could. . . . I myself would not want our love to be trumpeted through the streets, partly out of consideration for his wife, partly so that the sacredness of it not be sullied. . . . True, he wanted to introduce me in his house, make me his wife's friend, but understandably his wife wanted no part of this business, so that '*volens-nolens*' most of it had to be kept secret from her" (quoted in Carotenuto 1980, 12). Later in Jung's life, Antonia Wolff was taken into his home, and a triangle similar to the one Sabina describes was actually set up.

Spielrein writes of "the time our poetry began" (30) and says, "My friend [Jung] and I had the tenderest 'poetry' last Wednesday" (37). Carotenuto comments,

> For "poetry" we must surmise a metaphorical significance known only to Jung and Sabina. A literary analogy can be found in Proust. Swann and Odette used the metaphor *"faire cattleya"* [*cattleya* is a variety of orchid] to express the physical act of possession. (219)

So Carotenuto at least suspects that intercourse occurred, but this is not documented. Spielrein appealed to Freud to help free her from her attachment to Jung. Jung had excused himself by attributing his attraction to the brilliant young Jewess as a "transference" from his fascination with Freud's oldest daughter, Mathilde,[23] but the astute Sabina felt (quite rightly, I would guess) that it was Freud himself, not his daughter or Jung's wife, that was her real rival.[24]

This triangle involving a physician-friend who does something wrong with a female patient was potentially, for Freud, a reliving of the painful incident with his patient Emma Eckstein, whose nose Fliess had operated on in 1895 in Vienna on Freud's recommendation. After the operation, when Fliess had returned to Berlin, the woman had continued to hemorrhage and show signs of infection. The bleeding turned out to be not hysterical (Freud and Fliess's first assumption) but rather a result of Fliess's negligence in leaving a half-meter of gauze in the operation site, which had prevented healing. When this was removed by another surgeon, there was a hemorrhage that almost killed the patient. It was quickly stopped, and Freud

23. Jung was of course just learning about countertransference, but at Spielrein's emotional expense—he knew how disturbed she had been and put that aside to fulfill his own wishes; certainly the relationship went on too long to be able to excuse him much.

24. From a letter of Spielrein to Freud: "He [Jung] admitted he had excused his passion for me by speaking to you of the matter in terms of love for your daughter. . . . He wanted your [Freud's] love and therefore in his own defense grasped at the first plausible thing that entered his conscious mind upon hasty reflection, and which also appeared suitable to him in that particular situation because it would be pleasing to you. . . . Frl. Freud did not cause me the slightest jealousy: I was aware that Dr. Jung knew quite a number of intelligent women and would meet others, and I could clearly perceive her psychic kinship with me. The person who stood in my way was Prof. Freud himself" (Carotenuto 1980, 104–06).

grasped in an instant just what had happened; confronted with calamity, he felt sick. After her nose was packed, he "fled" into the next room to drink a bottle of water and thought himself pretty pathetic. As he returned "a little tottery" to her side, Emma Eckstein greeted him with the "superior" remark: "So this is the strong sex." (Gay 1988, 84)

Freud wrote to Fliess about his faintinglike reaction, "I do not believe that it was the blood that overwhelmed me—at that moment strong emotions were welling up in me" (1985, 117). "We can guess what they were," Gay adds. Fliess was blamed by others not only for the inexcusable malpractice of leaving in the gauze, but for operating at all. In his letter to Fliess about the operation, Freud initially exculpates the patient, but then blames first the gauze, then himself, then the Viennese surgeon Rosanes—all in the service of sparing—*not* blaming—his beloved Fliess.[25]

The similarity involved in Jung's malpractice in relation to Spielrein evokes the devil, who is clearly, and not only for Freud, partly Fliess. Jung complained that Spielrein has been spreading rumors about his "alleged" sexual misconduct:

> She has kicked up a vile scandal solely because I denied myself the pleasure of giving her a child. I have always acted the gentleman towards her but before the bar of my rather too sensitive conscience I nevertheless don't feel clean, and that is what hurts the most because *my intentions were always honourable.* But you know how it is—the *devil* can use even the best of things for the fabrication of filth. Meanwhile I have learnt an unspeakable amount of marital wisdom, for until now I had a totally inadequate idea of my polygamous components despite all self-

25. Freud: "So we had done her an injustice, she was not at all abnormal, rather, a piece of iodoform gauze had *gotten torn off* as you were removing it and stayed in for fourteen days, preventing healing, at the end *it tore off and provoked the bleeding.* That this mishap should have happened to you; how you will react to it when you hear about it; what others could make of it; how wrong I was to urge you to operate in a foreign city where you could not follow through on the case; how my intention to do my best for this poor girl was insidiously thwarted and resulted in endangering her life—all this came over me simultaneously. . . . I was not sufficiently clear at that time to think of immediately reproaching Rosanes. . . . You did it as well as one can do it. The tearing off of the iodoform gauze remains one of those accidents that happen to the most fortunate and circumspect of surgeons. . . . Of course no one is blaming you" (1985, 117–18; my italics). Freud was protesting too much.

analysis. Now I know where and how the *devil* can be laid by the heels. (207; my italics)

As if his confession were not sanctimonious enough, Jung tops it off with smugness:

These painful yet extremely salutary insights have churned me up hellishly inside, but for that very reason, I hope, have secured me moral qualities which will be of the greatest advantage to me in later life. The relationship with my wife has gained enormously in assurance and depth. (207)

In this letter, Jung asks Freud not to scold him "for my negligence" (209)—consciously he was referring to his not writing. Freud replies,

Many thanks for your telegram and letter, which (the telegram in itself did the trick) put an end to my anxiety. I evidently still have a traumatic hyperaesthesia toward dwindling correspondence. I remember its genesis well (Fliess) and should not like to repeat such an experience unawares. (209)

Freud, after invoking Fliess, goes on to reassure Jung about the rumors. (He did not know all the details which have been revealed by Carotenuto.) Again, concern for the woman/patient (obviously there in Freud's letters to Spielrein) took second place to concern for his friend and colleague. In his assuaging letter to Jung, Freud assumes the responsible role of devil,[26] quoting Goethe's Mephistopheles: "And another thing: 'In league with the Devil and yet you fear fire?' Your grandfather said something like that" (211). Jung was then just about to visit Freud. He writes back his own reassurance, which turned out to be a self-fulfilling prophecy expressed in negation:

You may rest assured, not only now but for the future, that nothing Fliess-like is going to happen. . . . It's just that for the last fortnight the devil has been tormenting me in the shape of neurotic ingratitude (letter of March 11, 1909, 211–12).

26. Freud, according to Carotenuto, was himself not completely above reproach in relation to Spielrein, although sexual impulses were not involved: He failed to fully acknowledge Spielrein's writings on the death instinct, which prefigured Freud's own theory.

Here the devil for Jung shifts from Freud and himself to the dispensable and seemingly already disposed of Fliess. Both men desired to deal with the distant rather than the recent past. Something "Fliess-like" had already happened in relation to Spielrein!

And something Fliess-like was going to happen again during Jung's visit to Vienna in April 1909: the theme of "spookery" blasts forth. Jung felt impelled to demonstrate his independence by, Mephisto-fashion, summoning up a kind of poltergeist to prove to Freud the reality of the occult and the possibility of predicting the future. The incident is described most tellingly by Schur, who comments on Jung's account of it:

> Curious to know Freud's general attitude toward "precognition and parapsychology," Jung claimed he raised the question with Freud, who allegedly characterized these concepts as "nonsense" out of "his materialistic prejudice." While Freud was developing his arguments, Jung had "a peculiar sensation" as though his diaphragm were made of iron which was starting to get red-hot—"a red-hot diaphragm vault." At the same moment there was such a crash in the bookcase standing beside them [Freud in his letter states it was in the next room] that both men became terribly frightened. Jung claimed that this was a "catalytic exteriorization phenomenon." When Freud protested against this "explanation," Jung predicted that another crash would follow shortly, and in fact it did. Jung never knew why he felt so sure of his prediction. As Freud looked horrified at all this, Jung (rightly) inferred that Freud had been left with feelings of distrust, and Jung himself felt that he had done something harmful to Freud. Jung claimed that he never spoke further to Freud about the matter. I would suspect, however, that Freud was more horrified at Jung's utterances than at the cracking sound in his bookcase! (1972, 251)

This should have shown Freud the depths of Jung's craziness. Freud was obviously very worried. Both men recognized what Jung calls "the Fliess analogy" (216). Freud apparently had been acting as analyst and had made some remarks about Jung's pregnancy fantasies, which may have precipitated the "neurotic ingratitude" of the analysand and the rebellious supernatural demonstration. Jung writes to repudiate Freud as father:

That last evening with you has, most happily, freed me from the oppressive sense of your paternal authority. . . . I hope I am now rid of all unnecessary encumbrances. Your cause must and will triumph, so my pregnancy fantasies tell me, which luckily you caught in the end. (218)

Freud responds, sadly but fondly, in a marvelous letter, telling Jung that he does not believe in the occult: "My credulity . . . vanished with the magic of your personal presence" (218). Freud provides a natural explanation of the predicted aural phenomena; he warns Jung against superstition[27] and links him with the numerologically obsessed Fliess by giving a long account of his own superstitious feeling about numbers, which Freud analyzes, removing any need for a supernatural explanation. For a while this exchange seems to clear the air. Jung writes Freud of the dangers of closeness in relation to his patient/colleagues Gross and Spielrein: "They are bitter experiences. To none of my patients have I extended so much friendship and from none have I reaped so much sorrow" (229). Freud uses Jung's reactions to demonstrate to him the power of countertransference, "a permanent problem for us" (231), but neither sees the parallel for their own relationship.

The prospect of a trip to America in response to invitations to both men from Clark University helps distance the unpleasantness about the spookery. The adventure of a journey to the New World, evoking the fantasy of two men on the road together that is common to adolescents (and had certainly been part of Freud's close emotional tie as a teenager to Eduard Silberstein), perhaps helped to discharge and sublimate the mutual temptations toward hostility and homosexuality. But the balance was precarious. Freud and Jung met in Bremen before the trip, and it was then that Freud suffered the first of his fainting fits in Jung's presence; it was a repetition of Freud's fainting[28] when he had met with Fliess. As

27. According to Jung (1961), during a meeting in Vienna "in 1910" (apparently a mistake for 1909), Freud warned him "never to abandon the sexual theory," which would be needed "as a dogma . . . an unshakable bulwark against the *black* tide of mud of occultism" (150; my italics). Jung regarded this as a demand for his faith (a demand that echoed those made by his minister father when Jung was a youth). The story links sexuality, anality (mud), the black man (minister father, devil) of Jung's fantasies, and occultism.

28. Jung also had been subject to what he calls "neurotic fainting fits" as a child, which he describes as starting at age twelve after another boy knocked him down, and he hurt his head on a curbstone. The fits occurred over a period of at least six

mentioned in chapter 6, Freud years afterward analyzed both as being associated with the theme of the murder of fathers and "an unruly piece of homosexual feeling" (Jones 1953, 317).

On the liner bound for America, Freud, Ferenczi, and Jung analyzed one another's dreams. It would seem that there was some discussion of homosexual impulses. However, in the correspondence between Freud and Jung, it is the passivity of *Ferenczi* that the two discuss. Most of their interpretations had to do with fathers and sons, but, as would be expected when male homosexuality is the topic, their dreams also led them to women: wives, sisters, mothers. Getting rid of fathers, wishes to love women, and the telling of the truth are themes interwoven in Jung's descriptive narrative, written long after the event:

> We were together every day and analyzed each other's dreams. . . . I regarded Freud as an older, more mature and experienced personality, and felt like a son in that respect. But then something happened which proved to be a severe blow to the whole relationship. Freud had a dream—I would not think it right to *air the problem* it involved. I interpreted it as best I could, but added that a great deal more could be said about it if he would supply me with some additional details from his private life. Freud's response to these words was a curious look— a look of the utmost suspicion. Then he said, "But I cannot risk my authority!" At that moment he lost it altogether. That sentence burned into my memory; and in it the end of our relationship was already foreshadowed. Freud was placing personal authority *above truth*. (Jung 1961, 158; my italics)

Right after this pronouncement, Jung tells of a dream of his that Freud tried to interpret. It was the famous dream that Jung wrote of elsewhere about the many layers of "my house" (Jung 1911–12). In the course of the interpretation, Jung decided to lie to Freud:

> What interested Freud in this dream were the two skulls. He returned to them repeatedly. . . . I knew perfectly well, of

---

months, and he was taken out of school. Jung describes overhearing his father tell a friend that the doctors suspected that Carl had epilepsy and that "it would be dreadful if he were incurable. I have lost what little I had, and what will become of the boy if he cannot earn his own living?" (1961, 30–31). Conflict over a father/son antagonism would appear to have been important in determining Jung's fainting fits as well as Freud's.

course, what he was driving at: that secret death wishes were concealed in the dream. "But what does he really expect of me?" I thought to myself. Toward whom would I have death wishes? I felt violent resistance to any such interpretation [but] submitted to [Freud's] intention and said, *"My wife and my sister-in-law"*— after all, I had to name someone whose death was worth the wishing! I was newly married at the time and knew perfectly well that there was nothing within myself which pointed to such wishes.[29] . . . I did not feel like quarreling with [Freud], and I also feared that I might lose his friendship if I insisted on my own point of view. On the other hand I wanted to know what he would make of my answer and what his reaction would be if I deceived him by saying something that suited his theories. And so I told him a lie. I was quite aware that my conduct was not above reproach, but *á la guerre, comme á la guerre!* (1961, 159–60; my italics)

Apparently victory in "la guerre" was to be placed "above truth" for Jung.

Some of the hidden meaning of this quoted exchange had been revealed (whatever the truth of the stories involved is) in an interview with Jung that took place in 1957, shortly before he wrote the account quoted above. Apparently Jung's reluctance to "air" Freud's "problem" in his book did not inhibit him during this interview. Jung told the interviewer, Professor John M. Billinsky, that when he and his young wife, Emma, first visited Freud in 1907, Freud was apologetic about his hospitality, saying, "I have nothing at home but an elderly wife" (Billinsky 1969, 42). Jung continued,

Freud's wife knew nothing about psychoanalysis [but] soon I met Freud's wife's younger sister. She was very good-looking and she not only knew enough about psychoanalysis but also about everything that Freud was doing. When, a few days later, I was visiting Freud's laboratory, Freud's sister-in-law asked me if she could talk with me. She was very much bothered by her relationship with Freud and felt guilty about it. From her I learned that Freud was in love with her and that their relationship was indeed very intimate. It was a shocking discovery to me, and even now I can recall the agony I felt at the time. . . . From the very beginning of our trip [to America] we started to analyze each

---

29. So much for a belief in the unconscious—or at least one's own!

other's dreams. Freud had some dreams that bothered him very much. The dreams were about the triangle—Freud, his wife, and his wife's younger sister. Freud had no idea that I knew about the triangle and his intimate relationship with his sister-in-law. (42)

The interview was published in the *Andover-Newton Quarterly* in 1969; its contents were picked up by national newsmagazines.

Jung's display in his autobiography of his relationship to the "truth" does not inspire confidence in view of his telling of these dreams related to wives and sisters-in-law and sexual triangles. The unlikelihood that "Aunt Minna" would make such a confession to a young man she had never met before hardly needs pointing out, and the notion of Freud's having had an affair with his sister-in-law has been dismissed as absurd by many who knew both (for example, personal communication from Max Schur, Freud's physician in the 1920s). In recent years Peter Swales has made much of the story, although not in a fashion that I find convincing. But, whatever the truth of the allegations, at least the fantasy of the affair was in the mind of Jung when he was remembering in old age, and the specific story does supply some basis for Jung's "lie": his answer of "wife and sister-in-law" to the question Freud asked him about the two skulls in Jung's dream.

I speculate that the triangle fantasy represents a projection onto Freud of Jung's own situation and, as we have seen, tendencies. By the time of this interview Jung had had an intimate relationship for forty years with a woman (Antonia Wolff) whom he had invited to share his home along with his wife. Billinsky (1969, 43) quotes Jung as saying, "It was my knowledge of Freud's triangle that became an important factor in my break with Freud." This would not have been the only time Jung retreated to two women in order to escape from his relationship with a father figure. The intimacy on the trip to America in 1909 also prefigures the break between the men in relation to fantasies about women.[30]

All the stress was covered over; the relationship had its more

---

30. The astute Carotenuto points out the parallel between Sabina Spielrein's "secret" letters to Freud about Jung, and Emma Jung's "secret" letters to Freud about her husband's relationship with him. Em*ma* (Jung's wife), Ir*ma* (the name Freud gave to Em*ma* Eckstein, whom Fliess operated on, *Ma*rtha (Freud's wife), *Mi*nna (Freud's sister-in-law)—all suggest ma*mma* and *Amme* (nurse). Both men, beneath and beside their "father complex," had basic problems relating to their

positive later times, but it was really deteriorating. Both Freud and Jung continued to deny that Jung was unable to transcend his conflict about paternal authority, and the men alternately provoked and defused their discord. Freud even tried intermittently to share Jung's belief in the occult in order to preserve the relationship. (Freud's ambivalent interest in the occult was an expression of a lifelong conflict, which persisted, partly as identificatory residue, long after the breaks with Fliess and Jung.)

Freud's main failing in relation to Jung was his narcissistic wish to have Jung be an extension of himself, especially to replace the part of his self-image that he felt was passive and inhibited. Jung was seen as a conquistador who would fight for Freud and psychoanalysis; Jung would fulfill Freud's libidinal, ambitious, and narcissistic wishes. The symbiotic claim (formerly brought to Fliess) did threaten Jung's separate identity. Since Jung seems not only to have feared but also to have longed to be swallowed up, he sensed the danger and temptation early on; but he could not control the intensity of his reactions. Freud was less threatened by his dominant role of father in the relationship than Jung was by the more passive one of son. But Freud seems to have been unaware of the depth of his involvement with Jung, and he insisted on projecting a need-fulfilling fantasy onto Jung in the service of denying their theoretical differences and the mutual emotional conflicts on which these were, in part, based. It is clear from Emma Jung's letters to Freud that she saw the dangers for both men in her husband's role as "son and heir." Jung's struggle for a separate identity (a struggle in his own mind as well as with Freud) is apparent throughout the correspondence. It is the preoedipal component (involving merger) of the central theme of the relationship—the Oedipus complex (involving submission or extermination or both).

Freud discovered oedipal wishes when he was analyzing patients and doing self-analysis in the 1890s. He announced his findings in a letter to Fliess of October 15, 1897. He early on recognized the universality of the sexual desire for the parent of the opposite sex and of the murderous hostility toward the parent of the same sex

---

mothers. Jung writes of how, when he was three, his mother "spent several months in a hospital in Basel, and presumably her illness had something to do with the difficulty in the marriage. . . . I was deeply troubled by my mother's being away. From then on, I always felt mistrustful when the word 'love' was spoken. The feeling I associated with 'women' was for a long time that of innate unreliability" (1961, 8).

and described it in *The Interpretation of Dreams* (1900). But it is in the years covered by the exchange of letters with Jung that Freud's insight deepens, and the Oedipus *complex* (as he first called it in 1910, borrowing the word from Jung) is seen as central in human behavior. At a time when his daughters and sons were approaching and attaining sexual maturity, Freud had been reliving his own Oedipus complex in its inevitable reversal of the parent/child roles with the onset of middle age. Much of this was involved in the relationship with son Jung: the father/son struggle with its inevitable intimations of homosexual surrender (the negative oedipal complex) as well as elimination of the rival.

Jung was not very sympathetic to the idea of the Oedipus complex. In early childhood, when he was the only child, his parents had not gotten along well. When he was four, his parents slept apart and the boy slept in his father's room. His father sometimes took the mother's place in caring for the young boy. But estrangement and enmity toward his father predominated as Carl grew older. When he was twenty, he watched his father die. His mother said to him cryptically, "He died in time for you" (1961, 96). Jung continues,

> The words "for you" hit me terribly hard, and I felt that a bit of the old days had come irrevocably to an end. At the same time, a bit of manliness and freedom awoke in me. After my father's death I moved into his room, and took his place inside the family. For instance I had to hand out the housekeeping money to my mother every week, because she was unable to economize and could not manage money. (1961, 96)

There was obviously much that was oedipal to be worked out that Jung resisted here.

The letters to Freud document Jung's need to run away from his emotional involvement with the "father creator" (279) by concomitantly repudiating the concept of the Oedipus complex. Jung defended against his feelings by generalization and abstract dilution: in his writings he treated incest as symbolic. He defended against his current situation with Freud and his past relation with his mother, his father, and the man who assaulted him sexually by displacing them to the distant and even the hypothetical past—he studied mythology. Meanwhile Freud was able in his writings to sublimate his involvement into understanding: he saw the connection between homosexuality and paranoia (the Schreber case,

1911); he competitively followed Jung's lead into mythological and historical studies but there too found a basic oedipal theme (*Totem and Taboo*, 1913).

It is easy to see in Jung's life that he seemed to have the need to find a father figure whom he would first worship and idealize and eventually rebel against, become disillusioned with, and, finally, despise and reject. This happened first with Bleuler and Janet and then with Freud. But each time there were variations in the intensity of the reactions, and, past his near psychotic episode following the break with Freud, Jung was able to modify and transform himself—and, presumably, the intensity of his need (without losing it). He learned something and strengthened his individuality.[31] There seems to have been a similar need to have two women (symbol of the mother according to Robert Fliess), a need probably enhanced in relation to his passive and submissive "feminine" wishes toward the father figure. Past the period of idealization of his wife (see Stern 1976, 71–76), Jung needed a woman besides his wife:

> He required a kind of double marriage, and its inherent tensions; only in such a triangle did he find safety and the intermittent intimacy he needed (Stern 1976, 76).[32]

This triangle was there with Sabina Spielrein and culminated in the long affair with Toni Wolff.

Both men, strongly tied to their mothers but consciously ob-

31. Stern: "The break with Freud, dreaded and wished for, was indeed a soul-shattering trauma that marked him for life. It threw him into a state of psychic desolation reminiscent of the sad years of his childhood. It shook the foundations of his being and hurtled him into a crazed agony of self-loss. It made him toil for a decade devising a typology that would transform his struggle with Freud into a matter of destiny, rooted in the fatalities of inborn character . . . While propelling Carl Jung toward his unique visionary reality, it exacted from him a heartrending tribute of loneliness. Never was Carl Jung more wretched, never more endangered by the incubus of madness, than after his break with Sigmund Freud" (1976, 112–13).

32. Stern continues, "In his essay [on marriage] Jung succumbed to the psychologist's eternal temptation: he unwittingly codified the rules regulating his own conduct as universal laws of human behavior. He seems to have managed, at any rate, to impose his law upon Emma [his wife], who came to accept the 'brutal reality' of the Jungian marriage. She was rewarded by Carl's gratitude and by being allowed to share in the gifts of his 'many-faceted' nature" (1976, 76; the quotes are from Jung's essay).

sessed with their fathers, were at this time led to study the importance of the mother, and Freud was now no longer calling the Oedipus complex the father complex. Indeed, the final break between Freud and Jung occurred in relation to the mother/child confrontation. For both sexes, analysis of homosexuality as well as of heterosexuality inevitably leads to the mother, the first representative experientially of the primal parent. Freud said in 1937 that a man's need to repudiate his femininity provides the "bedrock" (252) of his resistance to psychic change. But the hardest task is facing the feminine strivings (and the associated murderous impulses [see Shengold 1991]) in relation to the feelings that relate to the mother. Jung seems to recognize the problem. In February 1912, he apologizes for yet another delay in answering Freud's letters by explaining that he had been disturbed in his work:

> Essentially it is an elaboration of all the problems that arise out of the mother-incest libido, or rather the libido-cathected mother-imago. This time I have ventured to tackle the mother. So what is keeping me hidden is the katabasis [= descent] to the realm of the Mothers (487).

Here is another (*Faust*-derived) descent into Hell. But, following this connection of libido (sexual drive) with the mother, Jung is impelled in his lectures and writings to desexualize the concept of libido. Jung must attenuate the *experiential* quality of incest to "primarily a fantasy problem" (502) and ultimately to the symbolic and the mythical. The seduction by the father figure from childhood was suppressed, but the possibility of feeling and consummating sexual desire for the mother has to be denied. Jones writes,

> In May of [1912] Jung had already told Freud that in his opinion incest wishes were not to be taken literally but as symbols of other tendencies; they were only a phantasy to boost morale (1955, 163).

Shortly after Jung announces that he is "tackl[ing] the mother," he gets embroiled in a misunderstanding with Freud over what he calls the "Kreuzlingen gesture" (Jung had projected a slip he had made onto Freud).[33] Jung neglects his duties as president of the

33. Freud was planning to visit Binswanger at Kreuzlingen in Switzerland and wrote to Jung, whom he expected to meet him there. Jung did not show up. Jung then made sarcastic remarks which Freud found cryptic in letters that talked about

International Psycho-Analytical Association (as Karl Abraham keeps pointing out to Freud). Jung gives a series of lectures in America in which he dissociates himself from many of Freud's ideas. In November 1912, there is a very short-lived reconciliation at Munich during which Freud has another fainting fit. In December 1912 Jung's brutal letters bring an end to the personal relationship and correspondence.[34] *Faust* concludes with the Eternal Feminine, and these two spiritual sons of Goethe end their ties quarreling over the Mother and incest.

In response to Freud's pointing out a slip in one of Jung's letters in which he says "*your* group" instead of "*our* group," Jung dismisses Freud in a manner familiar to those who watch the mutations of the oedipal struggle. In his spite (his worst character traits are evident in these final letters), Jung still could not face the loss of a father; in order to get rid of Freud, he first reduces him to a brother:

> I am objective enough to see through your little trick. You go around sniffing out all the symptomatic actions in your vicinity, thus reducing everyone to the level of sons and daughters who blushingly admit the existence of their faults. Meanwhile you remain on top as the father, sitting pretty. . . . You see, my dear Professor, so long as you hand out this stuff I don't give a damn for my symptomatic actions; they shrink to nothing in compar-

---

"the gesture of Kreuzlingen." When they met later in the year in Munich, "Jung explained that he had not been able to overcome his resentment at Freud's notifying him of his visit [to Kreuzlingen two days too late]. . . . He had received Freud's letter on the day Freud was returning to Vienna. Freud agreed that this would have been a low action on his part, but was sure he had posted the two letters, to Binswanger and Jung, at the same time on the Thursday before. Then Jung suddenly remembered that he had been away that weekend. Freud naturally asked him why he had not looked at the postmark or asked his wife when the letter had arrived before levelling his reproaches; his resentment must evidently come from another source and he had snatched at a thin excuse to justify it. Jung became extremely contrite and admitted the difficult traits in his character" (Jones 1955, 164). Here was yet another confession and reconciliation. For both men this reenactment must have been a neurotic repetition, rather than a remembering, of the past. Jung repeats being with his parson father, and Freud (according to Jones) seems to have once again become optimistic about the relationship, characteristically encouraged by this reiteration of the return of the prodigal son.

34. There were some further exchanges on business matters but all friendship was over. Jung finally resigned as president of the International in early 1914.

ison with the formidable beam in my *brother* Freud's eye (535; my italics)

In 1920, long after Freud saw clearly what had been going on (at least on Jung's part) to cause the break, he added a note on the Oedipus complex to his *Three Essays* (originally published in 1905):

> It has been justly said that the oedipus complex is the nuclear complex of the neuroses, and constitutes the essential part of their content. It represents the peak of infantile sexuality, which, through the after-effects, exercises a decisive influence on the sexuality of adults. . . . With the progress of psycho-analytic studies the importance of the oedipus complex has become more and more clearly evident; its recognition has become the *shibboleth* that distinguishes the adherents of psychoanalysis from its opponents (1905, 226; my italics).

Jung was an opponent in 1920. Freud dismisses him here as if he were an Old Testament judge, making use of a favorite word, "shibboleth," with its connotations of murderous fraternal rage (see Judges 12:6).[35] Murder is of course also part of the Oedipus complex.

The Freud/Jung letters are a record of the relationship of two men of genius that is as fascinating and dramatic as any great novel. Their scientific split was predetermined by the nature of their oedipal conflicts (conflicts shaped as always by continuing pre-oedipal underpinnings). Jung could not master his and suffered a breakdown from which it took him years to recover. Donn (1988) reports that Jung's son Franz said to her, "My father would not confess it, but he probably never got over Freud in all those years" (27). Freud struggled in relation to Jung, as he had with Fliess, to consolidate the most difficult of all his insights. He was continuing his "interminable" self-analysis, a process he compared in a letter of 1900 to Fliess to the exploration of an intellectual hell (invoking Goethe but even more, Dante, another good hater)—a hell in which his parents and he himself were the demons frozen at the center.

---

35. The passage is about the war between the Gileadites and the Ephraimites, who were recognized by their difficulties in pronouncing certain words. If the captive denied being an Ephraimite, he would be tested: "Then they said unto him, Say now Shibboleth: and he said Sibboleth: for he could not frame to pronounce it right. Then they took him and slew him at the passages of Jordan: and there fell at the time of the Ephraimites forty and two thousand" (Judges 12:6).

Freud discovered that he was Mephistopheles as well as Faust; the devils were not without but within. For Jung, Freud had become the externalized black devil. And in Jung's struggle to achieve exorcism, Freud's insight—the fruit of the "tree of paradise"—was also cast out. Both men made use of each other and ultimately went on with identities enhanced by their contact.

FREUD AS EGO IDEAL AND AS
"A WHOLE CLIMATE OF OPINION"

> Freud was no angel, and he does not merit saint-
> hood. . . . I believe he was a man who could be cou-
> rageous, loyal, self-critical, candid, and generous.
> He could also be petty, catty, whining, cocky, opin-
> ionated, and stubborn. It appears that he may have
> been unfaithful to his wife, overly faithful to
> Wilhelm Fliess, and probably had blind spots when
> he was unhappy with clinical data not in accord
> with his own theories. He had the annoying habit
> described by Peter Gay as a "sovereign readiness
> to disregard his own rules." At the same time, his
> willingness and capacity to acknowledge his errors
> and forsake theories he so much cherished—and to
> accept that he had to start all over again along a
> particular line of thought—may be relatively
> unique in the history of science.
>
> —E. Weinshel, "What Does Freud and His Legacy
> Mean to a Contemporary Freudian Practicing
> Psychoanalysis?"

Weinshel's paper "What Does Freud and His Legacy Mean to a
Contemporary Freudian Practicing Psychoanalysis?" pays tribute to
Freud's major assumptions and ideas; he disputes a few; but it is
above all the set of Freud's mind in relation to his ideas that
Weinshel as a "Freudian" has taken over as his own. Despite Freud's
occasionally overweaning ways—part of his determination not to
be the boy who has come to nothing—he was so consciously dedicated to trying to find out "the truth—no matter what," that he
could frequently be (sometimes after great struggle) humble about

his ideas, change and shift them, and accept their inevitable deficiencies. To be a psychoanalyst should mean that one is able to be certain about some phenomena and ideas (clinical and theoretical) to the point of being willing to fight for their validity and yet recognize clearly the limits of one's knowledge and the enormous and inevitable place of uncertainty and mystery in human events. To obtain that state of mind—one in which narcissism is relatively severely suspended (if one is not lucky enough to start off with such a capacity before becoming a psychoanalyst)—it is necessary for the analyst to read and follow Freud's way of discovery and absorb his manner of holding onto and letting go of what has been discovered. This is perfectly consistent with having doubts about or rejecting some of Freud's ideas in the creation of one's own dynamic amalgam of psychoanalytic convictions and ways and with expecting that some of his and one's own ideas, techniques, prejudices will evolve, some will be superseded, and some will never be changed. But we must first know the history of psychoanalysis; that means *reading* Freud, learning not only what he said but, especially, how he said it and how he revised it.

Trilling (1961) comments on the relevance of Freud's personal history to the history of psychoanalytic thought:

> Like certain other disciplines, psychoanalysis is more clearly and firmly understood if it is studied in its historical development. But the basic history of psychoanalysis is the account of how it grew in Freud's own mind, for Freud developed its concepts all by himself. . . . That Freud should have been not only the one man who originated the science but also the one man who brought it to maturity is perhaps not wholly to the advantage of psychoanalysis. But such is the fact, and the narrative of Freud's life, of the intellectual difficulties he met and overcame, gives us a more intimate sense of the actuality of the psychoanalytical concepts than we can derive from the study of them as systematic doctrine, no matter how lucid are the expositions we read. And this, I believe is a pedagogic opinion which prevails in many of the institutes for the training of psychoanalysts. (12)

The prevalent pedagogic opinion has changed over the thirty years since Trilling wrote this. In the interim there has been much controversy about psychoanalytic education, and this reflects in some respects what has been going on, at least in the United States, in higher education in general. The debate in our specialized discipline is about the timing and the centrality of teaching Freud. The "traditional" method (psychoanalytic history is too short to eliminate the quotation marks) generally but not universally employed in the days when psychoanalysis was gaining and had achieved a major role in psychiatric education in America (the 1930s through the 1960s) was to study psychoanalysis historically (that is, chronologically). The curriculum would begin with Freud, starting from his earliest psychoanalytic writings and following them sequentially in order to study how his initial assumptions were modified, with other psychoanalytic contributors (such as Adler, Jung, Abraham, etc.) taking their chronological places until contemporary literature was reached. Some institutes still have this basic curriculum model.[1]

Psychoanalytic education was, and is, seen as a tripartite undertaking; the class curriculum I have described being one part; the analytic candidate's personal analysis another (optimally the most important) part; and (usually added when the candidate has shown evidence of competence and analyzability) the analytic work with patients performed by the student under the supervision of a training analyst, which is to justify the candidate's psychoanalytic education. The last two divisions of analytic training inevitably call forth a contemporary point of view. The complications of the individual human being's psychology as viewed in the dynamic arena of treatment bring up emotional conflicts centering on figures in the past now transferred onto the analyst in the present; and also the concomitant phenomena involved with defenses against transference impulses that come to current life and result in resistances to the analytic work. And, as each patient is different, the analyst is, in every case and in different ways, confronted with the limitations of analytic rules, theoretical generalizations, and those assumptions and that knowledge he or she has previously

1. Ideally Freud needs to be read first at or before the beginning of analytic training, so that the course of and changes in his ideas can be understood in a coordinated way; then re-read when the student has begun to do his own work as an analyst; and read again when some mastery of the work has been achieved after sufficient experience. This can be taken into consideration in a curriculum based on a model of spiraling repetition, with some of Freud's major papers, first approached in the first or second year, taken up again in the third or fourth and in postgraduate years. There would ensue not only increasing depth of understanding, but greater ability to criticize independently (as well as to appreciate or depreciate contemporary views of others).

held. For the student, both as patient and as analyst, the inevitable struggle with the unexpected usually results in some ability to coordinate past and present—in relation to one's own history, one's patients', and the history of psychoanalysis. The student must learn not only what can be known, but also what cannot be known, to arrive at a comprehension of the contradictions, complications, and mysteries of the human mind and the depth and complexity of the psychoanalytic point of view. Freud has led his students toward this evanescing goal.

Fortunately, the two clinical portions of psychoanalytic education have not been the subject of much argument and remain at the core of the training of psychoanalysts. But the historical approach to teaching theory and practice in the courses—reading Freud and his followers and opponents from the beginning on through—has been abandoned in many institutes in favor of starting with contemporary psychoanalytic writings that feature current synthesized views of clinical phenomena. Both approaches are legitimate and complementary; and either can be done well or badly. Ideally, Freud and the major talented psychoanalytic authors who followed him should be read both at the beginning of psychoanalytic education and again once the psychoanalyst has had experience of analysis both as patient and as analyst. One needs the perspective provided by seeing current intellectual and scientific achievement in the context of its evolution from what has been handed on from the past. Today's psychoanalysts stand on the shoulders of giants— with Freud as *the* super giant. They are human giants with faults; but in order to appreciate current positions and to challenge false certainties and defensive narcissistic feelings of omnipotence and superiority (summoned up to dispel the terrors of the unconscious and of one's inadequacies), students and practitioners of psychoanalysis must know how they have arrived where they are. Being able to grasp the relation between past and present is all important. The need of the student of the mind to read and know the great psychological thinkers of the past—specifically Freud—was more evaded than met by Otto Fenichel's conflatory compilation of the 1940s; and I fear this would be true for a contemporary equivalent. I repeat: having to know our history is a tenet of specific psychoanalytic as well as general wisdom. The aim of psychoanalytic treatment is to connect the dynamic emotional and ideational contents of the patient's conscious mind in the present with the unconscious traces from the past—again, to provide a meaningful perspective in time. If this "genetic" approach (that is, the exploration of where the patient, oneself and another, or both, have come from)—whatever the timing of its acquisition—is neglected and does not become part of the student analyst's functioning, psychoanalytic institutes will be turning out practitioners of current techniques rather than creative thinkers who can contribute to the evolution of the science and art of psychoanalysis.

The potential limitations of the historical approach are activated if Freud is presented as the possessor of Authority, of final wisdom whose word must be treated as some would-be "true believers" misguidedly regard the Talmud, as a sacred text whose contradictions and flaws must be justified and smoothed over. Since our basic unconscious motivations are contradictory, making us want both to idealize and to destroy our parents (authorities) and our heritage, we always have to fight off temptations from both directions. Freud-bashing and Freud-worship can arrive at the same obstructive end. In the course of a successful-enough personal analysis, the analytic patient who wants to go on to work as a psychoanalyst of others must free himself or herself insofar as it is possible from the automatic and unconscious needs to idealize and imitate, and to devalue and reject, authority and tradition—not only in relation to the training analyst (who has in the candidate's analysis become a parent and must go on to lose that status),[2] but in relation to Freud and to psychoanalysis itself. This requires the perspective, the honesty, and the acceptance of limitations and defects that are part of the psychoanalytic attitude set out by Freud.

In my office I have a photograph of Freud. It is in a bookcase, not in view from the couch; but it can be seen as one enters the office. One of my patients, Mr. H., expressed repeated outrage at my "weakness" in displaying such a picture in my office. How could I have such a deep need for a parental figure? Wasn't I ashamed to show such terrible dependency and let my patients see it? This patient turned out to be a victim of child abuse: seduced, overstimulated, used as an object to masturbate with, as well as tormented by his mother in nonsexual ways. The mother was presented as a crazy, dishonest woman whom the adult could describe

2. Part of analysis is the recapitulation of early development, with the analyst being felt not chiefly as the (idealized and beloved/devalued and hated) current parent but as representative of a dynamic series of earlier parental "objects," including the indispensable earliest parent figure who is regarded as part of one's self.

convincingly on the basis of memories that seemed to be fully
acknowledged as such, but in some way Mr. H. would easily put
aside what at first sounded like insight. There was a kind of more-
than-intellectual mental registration of specific and detailed events,
so that while Mr. H. could have given legal testimony about a good
deal that "undoubtedly" happened, the concomitant feelings
needed for true conviction were deficient. Remembering with feeling was unbearable. Reexperiencing the terrible combination of
overstimulation and murderous rage would bring to life the threat
of the loss of mother, and this meant overwhelming anxiety. Mr.
H. described in a voice full of irony how as a child he had thought
of his mother as being perfect. This was expressed with much
disdain toward his child-self, his voice full of the same emotional
tone he had used to condemn me for what he called my Freud
worship. He insisted that he had long ago been disillusioned and
could see his mother's faults, but it seemed apparent to me that his
old need to see her as perfect was still very much there. Mr. H. was
not at that time responsibly aware of how much he held onto his
deceitful, sadistic mother by becoming her. Every time he dupli-
cated her dishonest and sadistic attitudes and actions (the latter
usually in attenuation), he was, in his compulsion to repeat, unconsciously trying desperately but of course always in vain to assert
that this time mother and her ways would all come out good and
loving. The need to assert her benevolence, her perfection—the
intense need for idealization to preserve the mother—he projected
onto me in his delusional conviction about my relation to Freud.
(What one projects or externalizes is kept outside of conscious
critical awareness.) Mr. H. felt "intuitively" that Freud for me was
not just a respected leader or an ego ideal (he had done a good
deal of psychoanalytic reading) but a kind of exalted, deified "object" to whom I was in bondage and without whom I could not live.
The idealized image concealed a monster; and, late in the treatment, there was some ability to see me as the monster/parent whom
the patient himself could all-too-easily become.

As part of the torment Mr. H. endured as a child, his mother
had forced him to be the witness of her deceit, which included lying
and forgery. She had cultivated bad character in her child, and it
operated in him as an automatic, partly unconscious force. It was
not only that he was not to tell anyone about the dishonesty; he
was told that what he had seen had never happened, that *he* was a
liar. The result was a split of his mind into disconnected pieces:

part of him felt that she must be right, another that she was wrong and evil; he predominantly maintained that both he and his mother were blameless. To protect the relationship with his mother and spare her his murderous rage, the fragments were not integrated. This mother (as registered by her son and transferred and projected onto me in the analysis) seems to have been a living example of Robert Fliess's hypothetical phylogenetic parent out of Freud's primal horde (from *Totem and Taboo*, 1913) who returns in the mother or father who abuses the child as what Fliess calls the "archaic parent":

> Most pertinent . . . is the fact that the archaic parent shows in projection [of the patient-victim's superego onto the analyst] the same unvarying traits: the intent of torturing and killing, mendacity and lack of humor. (Fliess 1956, 39)

Mr. H. was, for the most part, gloomy and scowling, notably deficient in, but not quite incapable of, humor. When, toward the end of the analysis, Mr. H. was able to see responsibly the mendacious monster in himself, he did so in the course of contrasting me to his internist. He rather liked his internist, Dr. Y., although he didn't completely trust him. ("If you can't trust your mother, whom can you trust?") His internist had on his wall a picture of Einstein. Why, he asked himself, didn't that bother him in the way Freud's picture in my office did? Mr. H. was aware through his reading biographies of many imperfections and contradictions in Einstein's character. In contrast to what he had felt about me, Mr. H. was able to assume that Einstein was not an icon for his internist but just a great Jewish man who stood for wisdom. Why didn't he feel the rage and the conviction about my needing to worship Freud in relation to Dr. Y. and Einstein? I reminded him of what he had once told me: that whenever he had been physically ill his mother had taken good and reliable care of him. "Yes," he responded. "It is a wonder I didn't become a hypochondriac. I have always been in excellent health as an adult. And my mother was at her best as a nurse.[3] Maybe that's the difference. I don't feel I need my inter-

3. One often finds in the personal history of victims of what I have called soul murder (see Shengold 1989) that the abusing parent, especially perhaps the mother, has a vested interest in the child's illnesses and failures as representing regression toward the infantile state in which the child can be (and was) more easily regarded as a narcissistic extension of oneself.

nist that much. And I need you like I need my mother, God damn you!" "That's the way you feel that I need Freud," I replied.

This kind of connection had been made repeatedly before, but this time Mr. H. seemed able to make it his own. Later in the analysis, I chose to stretch ordinary analytic technique and share with him—it was after he had expressed (in a brief and transient regression) the old charges in relation to the picture of Freud—my view that the great man's portrait's presence in my office *was* a kind of idealization; but not his kind. His had been created on the basis of his intense, conflict-ridden, and desperate need to preserve his mother by denying those of her qualities and actions that made him want to hate and destroy her. I, too, was aware of some of Freud's human defects as well as of his enormous gifts and insights, but I wanted to have a picture of him in my office because I saw him as standing for the ideal of trying (at least in relation to one's predominantly benevolent work as an analyst) to get as close to the truth as possible, no matter what it cost; that I felt this ideal (so opposite to the attitude of Mr. H.'s mother) was part of the optimal functioning of a psychoanalyst. (Of course beneath my conscious helpful purpose and my aim at functioning with good character lurked my own personal failings and ambivalence that I had to be able to monitor and control in the service of the analytic ideal. Afterward my words, or rather my speech, and especially my attitude struck me as having been smug—none of this of course was communicated to Mr. H.) I did tell Mr. H. that what he felt obliged to put upon me with such conviction was his own terrible intensity of need to idealize in order to cover over his distrust and bad expectations.

It is not difficult to point out Freud's faults and failings. It is usually harder to face one's own. Every analysand successful enough to become able to achieve sufficient emotional openness and honesty to follow the analytic rule of saying what comes to mind becomes painfully aware of how much pettiness and narcissism, how much evil and destructiveness, how many blindspots and stubbornnesses, how many weaknesses in the face of temptation and of defensive need he or she has to face—and even has to retain after the analysis. The (frequently more difficult) ability to see some of the analyst's weaknesses and defects can and should also eventually be attained by the patient. This may not come until after the analysis itself.

The analyst's own personal analysis should prepare him, at least in relation to his work and patients, to function predominantly with the requisite good character, part of which is awareness of weaknesses and faults and honesty about them. This means the analyst's struggle with pride (Freud's was intense), evil, and falsehood—a struggle that cannot be completely successful but is for the most part relatively easy in the course of the primarily benign work done by the analyst. In the course of that work, the analyst can even make some use of unwarranted reactions to the patient—countertransference—since these, as long as one is aware of them, can frequently be of use in understanding what is going on in the patient. Good character is much harder to maintain in personal life. Any writer who leaves as much autobiographical evidence as Freud did—any great man whose life and records are examined closely enough by students and biographers—will easily furnish evidence of occasions that justify Hamlet's "Use every man after his desert, and who shall scape whipping?" (II.ii.555–56).

As Weinshel indicates, we know about Freud's difficulties with women, how unempathic he could be about and with his wife, how he was at times a soul-murdering Father Oedipus when he allowed himself to be the analyst of the daughter he called "my Antigone," how harsh he could be toward some women while overindulgent toward others, like the Princess Marie Bonaparte. The trouble he had integrating the role of the mother in early psychic development into his theory, his derogatory assumptions about the female genitals, his conviction about the inferiority of the woman's superego—these are well-known examples of how the conflicted passions beneath his personal weaknesses and blindnesses were reflected by lacunae and difficulties in his thinking and his theory ("What does Woman want?"). For years he underestimated in his theories the importance of the mother, of mothering, and of early (preoedipal) psychic development. (I am not trying to document all of Freud's deficiencies but am using a single important area—what Freud significantly called the "dark continent" of femininity—as demonstrating one cluster of them.) But Freud was consistently able to see many of his faults and failings—and even after having been inhibited and slow to see, was punctilious about acknowledging them. Freud made use of his female patients and colleagues to correct and modify many of his ideas and even some of his prejudices about women and their psychic development. He also showed a remarkable readiness, with whatever prejudices he retained, to change his opinions, his convictions, and his theories. He struggled manfully, with mixed but remarkably predominant success, to be able to do this.

Freud's mind proved broad enough not only to accept and accommodate facts contrary to his prejudices, assumptions, and theories but also to contain contradictions and be relatively comfortable (although not content) with the unknown and the unknowable. As evidence of his ability to change his mind about major theoretical and clinical assumptions, he often quoted from Charcot's reaction to facts that contradicted accepted wisdom: "La theorie, c'est bon, mais ça n'empêche pas d'exister" (Theory is a good thing but that doesn't prevent the facts from existing). Freud's characteristic ability to face being mistaken and to tolerate uncertainty with controllable anxiety was probably heightened by his self-analysis and the many surprising twists and turns of the discoveries he made in his early years as a psychiatrist and a psychoanalyst. Moreover the change of mind brought on by confrontation with unexpected clinical "facts" was often accomplished without Freud's feeling the need to give up old views completely. Instead he was able to see an increasing ambiguity and complexity in human events. For example, in the 1890s, motivated by his belief in his patients' stories of sexual abuse by adults in childhood, he had asserted in lectures and publications his "discovery" that traumatic sexual experiences in childhood, usually at the hands of a parent, were the causal factor in psychoneurosis. He had stated with consciousness of oversimplification and yet conviction that hysteria was the result of seduction by the father. Further contact with patients showed him that the stories, for most of his patients, were fantasies of having been seduced by parents. He reacted to his disillusion, after a short period of despair and consternation, with the discovery of the importance of fantasy life and of universal fantasies such as those involved in the Oedipus complex.[4] But that did not mean for him (as some have asserted) that incest and sexual

---

4. Here are excerpts from Freud's great letter to Fliess of September 21, 1897, that illustrate the pattern of discouragement followed by feeling heartened: "Now I want to confide in you immediately the great secret that has been slowly dawning on me in the last few months. I no longer believe in my neurotica [theory of the neuroses]. . . . So I will begin historically [and tell you] where the reasons for disbelief came from." There follows Freud's list, which includes "the certain insight that there are no indications of reality in the unconscious, so that one cannot distinguish between truth and fiction that has been cathected with affect. (Accordingly, there would remain the solution that *the sexual fantasy invariably seizes upon the*

abuse in childhood didn't actually occur and that its occurrence made no difference. Trilling (1961) comments that it was not just Freud's intelligence but a certain kind of moral force that was involved in his reaction in discarding his early theory of psychogenesis that had been based on his patients' stories:

> It was intelligence in the control of something else that went beyond anger at the deception and beyond chagrin at the ruined theory to ask why it was that all the patients told the same lie, to decide not to call it a lie but a fantasy, to find a reason for it, and to frame the theory of infantile sexuality. (16)

In 1926, when in late middle age, Freud's change of mind and theory in relation to anxiety led him to two different explanations for the origin of anxiety—two explanations he was unable to explain in a unified way. Anxiety arises both "automatically" from transformation of sexual energy in traumatic situations (which means it originates in the id) and as a signal of danger of a trauma (arising from the ego). Freud writes, "It will not be easy to reduce the two sources of anxiety into a single one" (1926a, 110). But he affirms that the two kinds and sources of anxiety exist and concludes with, "Non liquet" (It is not clear [1926a, 110]). What could not be settled he felt should be left in open mystery. (Leo Rangell has since presented a convincing way of resolving Freud's theoretical predicament.)

The felicitous ability to profit by changes in his convictions and opinions seems to have been further deepened by the wisdom arrived at in his last years. At any rate, in one of his last great papers, "On Constructions in Analysis," written in 1938 when he

---

theme of the parents.) . . . Now I have no idea of where I stand because I have not succeeded in gaining a theoretical understanding of repression and its interplay of forces. . . . If I were depressed, confused, exhausted, such doubts would surely have to be interpreted as signs of weakness. Since I am in an opposite state, I must recognize them as the result of honest and vigourous intellectual work and must be proud that after going so deep I am still capable of such criticism. Can it be that this doubt merely represents an episode in the advance toward further insight? It is strange, too, that no feeling of shame appeared—for which, after all, there could well be occasion. Of course I shall not tell it in Dan, nor speak of it in Askelon, in the land of the Philistines, but in your eyes and my own, I have more the feeling of a victory than a defeat (which is surely not right). . . . The expectation of eternal fame was so beautiful. . . . Everything depended upon whether or not hysteria would come out right. . . . In spite of all this, I am in very good spirits" (Freud 1887–1904, 264–66, my italics).

was eighty-two and in great pain from his cancer, he gives an eloquent presentation of what is an essential characteristic of the psychoanalyst. It is a statement about constructions (that is, the analyst constructs or reconstructs a meaningful linkage that is induced from the patient's associations—a hypothesis about past events or tendencies that the patient does not or cannot remember). Whether the hypothesis will stand will ultimately depend on the patient's reaction, but

> these [initial] reactions [to the analyst's constructions] on the part of the patient are rarely unambiguous and give no opportunity for a final judgement. Only the further course of the analysis enables us to decide whether our constructions are correct or unserviceable. We do not pretend that an individual construction is anything more than a conjecture which awaits examination, confirmation or rejection. We claim no authority for it, we require no direct agreement from the patient, nor do we argue with him if at first he denies it. In short, we conduct ourselves on the model of a familiar figure in one of Nestroy's farces—the manservant who has a single answer on his lips to every question or objection: "It will all become clear in the course of future developments." (1938b, 265)

This statement, with its quotation from Nestroy, the Austrian writer of farces whom Freud so often quotes in his papers and in his letters, concerns validation, certainty, and uncertainty. Freud supplies here an injunction to the analyst concerning his technique: how to conduct himself in relation to the patient. Although Freud is specifically speaking of constructions (in current psychoanalytic literature usually called reconstructions), what he says could apply to any interpretation or connection that the analyst makes for the patient. If, as Freud describes, conjecture is to be turned into conviction, conviction (although arrived at in the interplay between patient and analyst) is ultimately up to the patient. The patient's conviction is dependent in large part on how the functioning of his unconscious mind has been determined and whether it is subject to modification in the establishment—*if* it can be established—of what is for him emotionally true. What eventually counts in an analysis is not the analyst's but the patient's conviction—the patient's being able to own the new connection or fact. And the analyst must always be aware of the possibility of false conviction on the part of either or both participants in the treatment. There is no simple way to connect with authentic emotional involvement the past and the present, yet making this connection is the essence of psychoanalytic work. The authenticity and conviction are usually arrived at by way of the long and difficult struggle between patient and analyst and in the mind of the patient (the patient's resistances): a struggle inherent to the coming to full conscious vitality of conflictual, emotion-laden aspects of the patient's dynamic fantasy life (derived from fantasy and experience from the past) that get transferred onto the person of the analyst in the present. (Freud equates elements of unconscious fantasy vitalized by the transference onto the analyst in psychoanalysis with "ghosts in the underworld of the Odyssey—ghosts that awoke to new life as soon as they tasted blood." The patient's feelings toward the analyst supply that blood, primarily in relation to him or her as a new object for the patient's old instinctual—sexual and aggressive—wishes, and partly in the form of taking in the analyst as a model and ideal.)[5]

I honor Freud as an ideal not only in relation to his attitude toward the truth and his broadness and flexibility of mind but also for his stoicism and courage. He was a man who was, relatively speaking, unafraid of the force of the conventional. Once, in response to Ferenczi's suggestion in a letter that Freud "closely re-

---

5. New knowledge was acquired and new models evolved, especially as Freud examined what was going on between his patients and himself—the patients' transferences, projections, and resistances and Freud's reactions to these. No one is better than Lawrence Friedman in clarifying Freud's historical course of sequences of mutually influenced changes in theoretical concepts and technical measures based on the interplay between theory and practice that was initiated so often by Freud's musing on what he saw in his work with analytic patients. In a paper entitled "A Reading of Freud's Papers on Technique" (1991), Friedman writes, "Freud's *Papers on Technique* is the canonical description of the psychoanalytic procedure. It is a puzzling work because it is dominated by the original paradigm of treatment as memory-retrieval, while at the same time it introduces a new picture, more consistent with Freud's emerging theory of passions, according to which treatment is the stirring up and integration of wishes. I suggest that *Papers on Technique* becomes less puzzling if we assume that, when he wrote it, Freud was mainly concerned not with theory but with a crucial problem of practice. In exchange for some theoretical inconsistency Freud acquired an important practical advantage, and *Papers on Technique* uses that advantage to teach analysts how to divide the patient's consciousness into a passionately committed experience, on the one hand, and a detached contemplation, on the other hand, without worrying about the element of manipulation that is involved. The lesson is that a theoretical ambivalence of this sort is essential to the analytic stance" (564).

sembled Goethe" (Jones 1955, 182), Freud stated his reaction to this comparison to one of his main ego ideals:

> I really think you are doing me too much honor, so that I get no pleasure from your ideas. I do not know of any resemblance between myself and the great gentleman you cite, and that not because of modesty. I am fond enough of the truth—or let us rather say of objectivity—to dispense with that virtue. . . . Let me admit that I have found in myself only one attribute of first quality: a kind of courage that is not affected by conventions. (Jones 1955, 182–83)[6]

Freud's courage was operative not only in relation to ideas and intellectual matters. The boy who wanted to be Hannibal, rescuer of his father, was determined to be courageous physically, and he was frequently able to achieve this goal. Peter Gay cites many instances of Freud's pugnaciousness and physical courage that were specifically evoked by antisemitic words and actions of Christians (Freud's reactions were so in contrast with his father's timidity in this regard). He was able even to be slyly defiant to the Nazis, adding on to the statement of exoneration he was forced by the Gestapo to sign before being granted an exit visa from Austria the sentence "I can heartily recommend the Gestapo to anyone" (Jones 1957, 226).

Trilling pays homage to Freud's intellectual achievement as a moral achievement that involved the need to defy conventionality in his professional world—a defiance that required the kind of courage that in our slang we can appropriately put in physical terms: guts or balls:

> One has reference to the courage of a man in middle life,[7] with family responsibilities and a thoroughly conventional notion of how these must be met, who risked his career for the sake of a theory that was anathema to the leaders of his profession. It

6. Contrast Freud's modest assertion of his tolerance of immodesty with the idolatrous tone of Jones's praise of Freud's honesty later in this chapter.

7. Trilling points out that Freud's dreams of achievement, his determination to be a genius, "were fulfilled relatively late, that his characteristic powers did not manifest themselves until middle life. . . . If we take the case of Fraulein Elisabeth von R. as being the first clear indication of what Freud was to do, and if we take the date of that case as 1892 . . . , Freud was thirty-six before he began to do the work that made him famous" (1961, 14–15).

was reprobated not merely on the grounds of respectable morality, although these were compelling enough, but also on intellectual grounds—Freud's ideas challenged the scientific assumptions on which German medicine had made its very considerable advances. To men of the school of Helmholtz, the idea that the mind—not the brain, not the nervous system—might itself be the cause of its own malfunction, and even the cause of the body's malfunction, was worse than a professional heresy: it was a profanation of thought. It was in the tradition of these men that Freud had been trained and it was this tradition that he was expected to continue and ornament. In point of fact he never wholly repudiated it, for he affirmed its determinism while negating its materialism, but what he did deny raised against him a storm of outrage which he met with a magnificent imperturbability. (1961, 15)

Trilling points out here Freud's challenge to the fathers. He dares, heartened by his feeling that he is backed up by the clinical evidence, unpleasant though this may be, to show his phallic power and let his own creative stream flow defiantly—to urinate, as it were, in their presence and even to urinate on them. There is also a reminder here of Freud's ability to model himself on (without imitation or loss of his own individuality) and derive sustenance from these intellectual fathers. This mirrors in the intellectual realm much of the ambivalence of the son's involvements with and derivations from Jacob Freud.

If his life did not in other ways frequently involve the need to conquer physical fear expected of the ideal conquistador, Freud did demonstrate a continuing, remarkable bravery in facing in late middle and old age the fact and the experience of death—his impending own and that of beloved others. And Freud characteristically (that is, throughout his life) was able to confront terrible blows of fate—but these came rushing on in his old age when "by a series of events the cruel and irrational nature of human existence was borne in upon him with a new and terrible force" (Trilling 1961, 18).

One sees, as one reads him, how broad his mind was . . . but far more affecting than his breadth of mind is the spectacle we receive from his last essays of the steadfastness with which he bore his increasing loneliness, his frequent bouts of pain, and the dangers of his disorderly time: conditions which provided him with a limitless testing-ground, on which he learnt to accept the ineluctable facts of life and death, and to feel his way towards what lies beyond them. (Cohen [1958], on Michel de Montaigne)

This praise of Montaigne could have been written about Freud's last years and last writings. Some of the most admirable aspects of Freud's character—qualities that go into our use of him as an ego ideal—emerge most fully during the time of his old age, the time of writing the book on Moses, his last essays, and the *Outline of Psychoanalysis;* the time of the repeated operations for the cancer that left him in so much pain; the time of the Nazis and his need to flee from his beloved and hated Vienna to England.

There is a good deal of resemblance between the minds of Sigmund Freud and the great philosopher Montaigne ("The world is but a school of inquiry" [Montaigne 1580–92, 295]); both men reached for general psychological truths by way of self-scrutiny—by "prob[ing] the workings of the passions in their inner lives" (Gay 1988, 129). Much could be said of the similarity of the two men's attitudes toward women; a parallel could be made between the relationship of Montaigne and his older friend Etienne de La Boétie and that of Freud and Fliess—although they ended so differently.[8] In 1576, when he was forty-three, Montaigne had a medal forged that served as a kind of talisman expressing the intentions of the *"essais"* (= trials of thought) that were becoming his life's work. On one side he had engraved, *"Que sçais-je?"* (What do I know?); on the other, *"Je m'abstiens"* (Restraint!). These are certainly

---

8. From Montaigne's "On Friendship"; he is speaking of the relationship between women and men: "Moreover, the normal capacity of women is, in fact, unequal to the demands of that communion and intercourse on which the sacred bond [of friendship] is fed; their souls do not seem firm enough to bear the strain of so hard and lasting a tie. And truly, if that were not so, if such a free and voluntary relationship could be established in which not only the soul had its perfect enjoyment, but the body took its share in the alliance also, and the whole man was engaged, then certainly it would be a fuller and more complete friendship. But there has never been an example of a woman's attaining to this, and the ancient schools are at one in their belief that it is denied to the female sex" (1580, 95).

Montaigne's intense relationship with La Boétie lasted for five years until the premature death of the latter, and "his influence lasted with his younger friend til the end of [Montaigne's] life" (Cohen, 15). Montaigne makes it explicit that the bond was not sexual. He writes of the two men's minds mixing "in so perfect a union that the seam which has joined them is effaced and disappears. If I were pressed to say why I love him, I feel that my only reply could be: 'because it was he, because it was I'" (1580–92, 97).

also Freudian mottos. Freud saw how the analyst must be aware of his own needs, wishes and neurotic patterns, so that these can be restrained in relation to the patient who so readily presents himself or herself as the vulnerable child who would do anything to reassert the infantile promise of achieving everything through contact with the parental figure. The analyst must, like the good parent, forego his or her own satisfactions; the analyst is not to try to gratify or to reenact his or her neurotic wishes with the patient. The analyst aims for a benevolent neutrality centered on using his knowledge of himself and others to help face what is there in the patient's mind and world. This again involves trying to serve that difficult-to-define abstraction: what is true.

Freud returned to this Montaignian theme once more in old age when he took up the figure of Akhenaten (Abraham's Ikhnaton) in *Moses and Monotheism*. (Freud's suppression of Abraham's part in his thoughts—connected by me with Freud's mixing him up with his consciously abandoned ego ideal Fliess—would represent the effect of that directly opposite part of Freud's unconscious mind that needed to break with the truth and to hold onto, partly through identification, Fliess as the devil, the bad and mendacious primal parent.)

Jones (1955, 426) points out Freud's identification of himself with "Akhenaten [who] boasted of his joy in the creation and of his life in Ma'at [the goddess of truth, order and justice]" (Freud 1939, 59). Akhenaten was an ego ideal of Freud's Moses and of Freud. Freud wrote,

> The Egyptian Moses had given to one portion of the people a more highly spiritualized notion of god, the idea of a single deity embracing the whole world, who was not less all-loving than all-powerful, who was averse to all ceremonial and magic and set before men as their highest aim a life in truth and justice. For, however incomplete may be the accounts we have of the ethical side of the Aten religion, it can be no unimportant fact that Akhenaten regularly referred to himself in his inscriptions as "living in Ma'at" (truth, justice). (1939, 50)

Here is Jones's descriptive panegyric:

> Honesty with Freud was more than a simple natural habit. It became an active love of truth and justice—the Goddess Maat of whom he wrote so warmly in his last book—and brought with it

an equally strong dislike of any deception, ambiguousness or prevarication. Even the simplest form of compromise, a quality that would certainly have made his life easier, was anathema to him. He went so far here as to develop a dislike of the usual formalities of social relationships, conventional or otherwise, and laid little store by the common graces of life. (1955, 426)

One feels Jones portrays Freud as too good, but perhaps not too good to be true.

Trilling writes of the moral force that colored Freud's undoubtedly sincere feelings about the inadequacy of his intellectual endowment, feelings that seem so ludicrous in the light of his achievement. This sense of insufficiency, surely a neurotic failing connected with "The boy will come to nothing," Freud was able, frequently through heroic struggle, to turn to creative account. Trilling says,

> Yet Freud is describing an actuality. However intellectually brilliant his developed ideas now seem, they did not *feel* brilliant as he conceived them; the feeling was rather that of patience, of submission to facts, of stubbornness. Pride in every good sense of the word, was a salient quality of Freud's temperament. But he reached his discoveries by means of thought which walked no less humbly than courageously. The humility of the scientist, his submission to facts, is something of which the scientist often boasts, but the facts to which Freud submitted were not only hard but also human, which is to say disgusting, or morally repellent, or even personally affronting. (1961, 16)

One can glean from Trilling's remarks a "compromise formation" for Freud involving his creative transformation ("sublimation") of the potentially pathological passivity marked transiently by his conflicts, symptoms (fainting fits), and inhibitions (manifestations of his feelings of inferiority and self-doubt). This pathology flowered in the periods of Freud's masochistic submission to the person and ideas of Fliess and even of Jung. Passivity is the component of bisexuality which for the male is, in Freud's view, the "bedrock" which can mark the limit of what psychoanalytic treatment can effect. Yet Freud's "submission to facts" became for him a great source of his feeling of authenticity and identity as well as of creative and aggressive power. I conclude that there are complex and individually differing balances between neurosis and health, between passivity and aggressiveness, between pride (Freud's was immense) and humility, healthy egoism[9] (narcissism) and an ability to care for others—and that some such pliant, optimal balances of contradictory or contrasting qualities are components of or preconditions for creative sublimation in any individual. I feel further that with Freud the qualities of his mind involved in the way he worked out his ideas, the process of their derivation, is at least as important to his identity and to his genius as the ideas themselves. To characterize it with a well-known saying of Montaigne's, "The journey, not the arrival, matters."

Montaigne was tortured but not thwarted by gall bladder colic in his later years; Freud was similarly affected by his buccal cancer. Both men kept writing and thinking up to the end, accepting their aging, failings, and great physical pain—as well as the turmoil in the world around them—with heroic stoicism and ferocious honesty (Montaigne: "I find in old age an increase of envy, injustice and malice" [1580, 250]). Trilling says, "Reading [accounts] of [Freud's] late and last years, we ask . . . 'This ageing man, this old man, this dying man—will he possibly remain Sigmund Freud?' He did, and the record of his endurance not in mere life but in his own quality of life makes one of the most moving of personal histories" (1961, 17–18).

Trilling writes of these years of pain and loss, persecution and exile:

> In 1923 [at age sixty-seven] he learned that he had cancer of the jaw. Thirty-three operations were to be performed, all sufficiently harrowing, and for sixteen years he was to live in pain, often of an extreme kind. The prosthesis he had to wear was awkward and painful, distorting his face and speech, and he was, as we know, a man of some vanity. ("My prosthesis doesn't speak French," he said in touching apology on the occasion of a visit to Yvette Guilbert.) . . . Yet nothing breaks him and nothing really diminishes him. He often says that he is diminished, but he is not. He frequently speaks of his indifference. But the work goes on. . . . At his death he is still working on his "Outline of Psychoanalysis." He continues with his clinical work up to a

9. Trilling: "His own egoism led him to recognize and respect the egoism of others" (1961, 20). True, but this is far from common, and the how and why of it for Freud remains mysterious.

month before his death. And nothing abates the energy and precision of his personal relationships. (1967, 3)

After a lesion in his mouth was discovered in 1923, Freud had a terrible, badly managed operation in which he almost bled to death postoperatively. His personal physician of long standing (Felix Deutsch) and his surgeon (Hajek) did not tell Freud or anyone in his family that cancer had been found. X-ray treatment was then prescribed, and six months later another operation was determined on. Then Freud was told of his having been deceived as to the diagnosis, and he indignantly dismissed Deutsch and replaced Hajek by Professor Pichler, who was to remain Freud's surgeon over the next fifteen years.

Shortly after his first operation, Freud suffered a terrible and completely unexpected tragedy—his favorite grandchild, Heinele, a charming and brilliant four-year-old, suddenly became very ill and died from tubercular meningitis. Freud wrote, "I find this loss very hard to bear. I don't think I have ever experienced such grief" (quoted by Schur 1972, 358). Schur adds,

In a letter to Ferenczi written [a month after Heinele's death], Freud declared that he was suffering from 'the first depression in my life.' Afterward he remarked repeatedly that this event had killed something in him, so that he was never able to form new attachments. (1972, 359)

Four years after letting Deutsch go, there was an interim during which he relied on Pichler, his surgeon, not only to perform more operations but also to check on his condition and his prostheses. There was torment involved in the reliance on the prostheses; not one of them was satisfactory, and they became increasingly difficult to put in and take out. In 1928, when Freud was seventy-two, he finally consented to take on a personal physician again. His friend, pupil, and patient, Marie Bonaparte recommended the thirty-two-year-old Max Schur. Schur was to remain Freud's personal doctor for eleven years. In constant attendance, he, with Freud's daughter, Anna, looked after the daily prosthesis insertion ritual, and he presided over Freud's death. Schur describes their first meeting:

There was nothing patronizing in this meeting of the sage master with a young doctor more than 40 years his junior. While I could not miss the searching quality of those wonderfully expressive eyes, he put me immediately at ease by acknowledg-

ing his appreciation of the way I had handled the treatment of
Marie Bonaparte. In the shortest possible time, he showed his
readiness to establish a patient-doctor relationship based on mutual respect and confidence. Before telling me his history or his
present complaints, he wanted a basic understanding for such a
relationship. Mentioning only in a rather general way "some
unfortunate experiences with your predecessors," he expressed
the expectation that he would always be told the truth and
nothing but the truth. My response must have reassured him
that I meant to keep such a promise. He then added, looking
searchingly at me: . . ."Promise me one more thing: that when
the time comes, you won't let me suffer unnecessarily." All this
was said with the utmost simplicity, without a trace of pathos,
but also with complete determination. We shook hands at this
point [1972, 408]. . . . Never did I hear an angry or impatient
word directed against anyone around him, and for the last few
weeks of his life I lived in his home! (413)

Trilling speaks of the constructive power of Freud's pride and
his narcissism which were components of his moral passion:

He may indeed have been, as he said, indifferent to his own
life, to whether he lived or died. But so long as he lived, he was
never indifferent to himself. And this, surely, is the secret of his
moral being. He had the passionate egoism, the intense pride
that we call Titanic. *"Mit welchem Recht?"* ("By what right?"), he
cried, his eyes blazing, when Dr. Jones told him in London that
at the time the diagnosis had first been made, there had been
some thought of concealing from him the truth about his cancer.
He is very old, the episode is now long in the past, yet he springs
to instant anger at the mere thought that his autonomy might
be limited. (1967, 3)

Schur reports that Freud would not use analgesic drugs and only
took some aspirin toward the very end. He told Schur that he would
rather think in torment than not be able to think clearly.

Freud, the only parent, as it were, of psychoanalysis, tends to
become therefore a model—for each the idiosyncratic, individually
formed model—for the ego ideal of the psychoanalyst. The impact
of his personal qualities as evidenced in his life and especially in
his writings influences each of his descendants—directly as he is
perceived and assimilated as a kind of ancestor and indirectly

through the medium of those qualities transformed and re-formed by the person of the training analyst—the analyst (who has a similar impact on his patient) of the future analyst. These influences in turn have an impact on the analyzed analyst's patients. So the qualities of Freud's mind and character can be felt, in some diluted and transfigured way, by all analysands.

In any psychoanalytic treatment that works, the psychoanalyst is used as a target for identifications, transferences, and projections. The analyst becomes an increasingly important other who is transformed (at first transiently but eventually in a more structured and permanent, but still dynamic and shifting) way into part of the patient's self—part of the conscience and of the ego. This takes place by taking into the mind at first aspects of the patient's own mental representations of self and of parental (and other) figures who are unconsciously projected and transferred onto the analyst. Features of the analyst's real self and especially of his functioning as the analyst (optimally with the good, Freud-like, broadminded, nonjudgmental, unselfish, truthful moral qualities I have described) begin also to be taken in and identified with. The analyst fosters this kind of potentially structure-enhancing and transforming identification by doing his or her best not to make narcissistic, libidinal, and aggressive claims on the patient. These claims not only sully the clarity of what is going on in the mental world of the patient, they also tend to repeat the past and interfere with the patient's power of deciding the future. If these countertransference interferences do arise in a way that compromises the analytic work, the analyst should deal with them honestly in his or her mind—and also, when indicated (the analyst may be aware that they are there without feeling that they are operative),[10] openly. In the course of an analysis, the analyst draws out preoedipal and oedipal wishes, becomes primal parent and is split into mother and father, and also plays the role of those (real, historical, mythical, fictional) others who have subsequently taken over as parental derivatives and substitutes. Eventually the benevolent, relatively neutral, and firm but flexible functioning of the analyst can become a model for a simi-

10. Timing and tact are important: on the one hand the patient should have achieved some readiness to deal with the analyst's countertransference; on the other hand, some manifestations are evident and must be discussed openly. How much and what to discuss are of course a matter for the analyst's discriminatory empathic skill.

larly functioning—I would like to emphasize *flexible* (but substantial)—ego ideal, one that can be modified or even temporarily lost without terrible guilt, shame, or danger. The analyst's picture (and also grandfather[11] Freud's picture) can be put up on one's psychic wall, but it must also become transiently removable and even replaceable. There should be not just one but many pictures on that hypothetical wall; their preeminences shifting. Their flexible use can help furnish perspective, tolerance, humor, courage, and other qualities of character that contribute to the dilution of primitive narcissism—enhancing the ability to care for others as part of caring for oneself.

Freud was born in 1856. After 1900 he began to acquire followers. He was awarded an honorary degree from Clark University in America in 1909, his first official international recognition. Freud's psychiatric followers in the German and Austrian armies in World War I used psychoanalytic techniques on shell-shocked soldiers and impressed their governments with its effectiveness. The popularity of his writings spread, and Freud emerged from the intellectual isolation of his early years.

In the 1920s, Freud was beginning to be, to paraphrase Yeats, a sixtyish-year-old smiling public man, just entering on his international fame. (The cancer that was to interfere with his smile was discovered in 1923.) But in these years of personal tragedies and illness, Freud's ideas were taken up by psychological scientists, artists, and intellectuals in Austria, Germany, England, France, Italy, and America. By the end of the decade *The Interpretation of Dreams* and most of Freud's other works had been translated into many languages. The Goethe Prize came in 1930. By then would-be pupils and patients had for some years been flocking in from all over the world. By the time he died in 1939 Freud was a household name, and in psychological science and the worlds of the arts and the universities he had indeed become "a climate of opinion." His views on childhood sexuality, although frequently misunderstood

11. Grandparents can be strong contributors to ego ideal formation—they are frequently a benevolent and tempering force. (Of course this is not always so; there are power-hungry, malevolent, crazy, soul-murdering, criminal grandparents too—like Gorki's grandfather.) They can love at a greater emotional distance since they usually don't have either the primary responsibility for care or the intense narcissistic investment of the parents. The distance also makes it easier for the child to idealize them—but of course also to scapegoat them in displacement from the parent.

and misused, had pervaded the ways people in the Western world
brought up their children. Biography and literary criticism were
radically (and again—initially—not always happily) affected. Training institutes had been set up in the major capitals of Europe and
America and were profoundly influencing psychiatric thinking and
practice. Freud had become a genius-cliché, like Einstein—two
Jewish boys who were popular demigods, worshiped but mocked,
the source of authority as well as the subject of caricature. In his
old age "the boy" had indeed become a somebody, belying his
father's transient, angry, reactive prophecy.

Freud as a grown man had several dreams (the "Count Thun"
and "open-air closet" dreams) involving urination and great ambition that were included in *The Interpretation of Dreams* (1900). In the
"open-air closet" dream, Freud sees himself as a giant and a hero—
as Hercules, with associations to Gulliver and Gargantua. Here are
the dream and some of Freud's associations:

> A hill, on which there was something like an open-air closet:
> a very long seat with a large hole at the end of it. Its back edge
> was thickly covered with small heaps of faeces of all sizes and
> degrees of freshness. There were bushes behind the seat. I
> micturated on the seat; a long stream of urine washed everything
> clean; the lumps of faeces came away easily and fell into the
> opening. It was as though at the end there was still some left.
>
> Why did I feel no disgust during this dream?
>
> Because, as the analysis showed, the most agreeable and sat-
> isfying thoughts contributed to bringing the dream about. What
> at once occurred to me in the analysis were the Augean stables
> which were cleansed by Hercules. *This Hercules was I.* The hill
> and bushes came from Aussee, where my children were stopping
> at the time. I had discovered the infantile aetiology of the neu-
> roses and had thus saved my own children from falling ill. The
> seat (except, of course, for the hole) was an exact copy of a piece
> of furniture given to me as a present by a grateful woman
> patient. It thus reminded me of how much my patients
> honoured me. . . . The stream of urine which washed everything
> clean was an unmistakable sign of greatness. It was in that way
> that Gulliver extinguished the great fire in Lilliput—though
> incidentally this brought him into disfavour with its tiny queen.
> But Gargantua, too, Rabelais' superman, revenged himself in the

same way on the Parisians[12] by sitting astride on Notre Dame and turning his stream of urine upon the city. It was only on the previous evening before going to sleep that I had been turning over Garnier's illustrations to Rabelais. And strangely enough, here was another piece of evidence that I was the superman. . . . The fact that all the faeces disappeared so quickly under the stream recalled the motto: '*Afflavit et dissipati sunt*' [He blew and they were scattered], which I intended one day to put at the head of a chapter upon the therapy of hysteria. (468–69)

Freud attributes the dream to praise he received after giving a lecture the afternoon before the dream from a member of the audience: "telling me how much he had learnt from me, how he looked at everything with fresh eyes, how I had cleansed the Augean stables of errors and prejudices in my theory of the neuroses. He told me, in short, I was a very great man" (470). This praise had irritated Freud. He had also dipped into Rabelais before going to sleep that night.

In wishing to be Hercules, the adult dreamer Freud sees himself as a hero who embodies fulfillment of conscious and unconscious, allowed and forbidden, and conflicting wishes he had had as an oedipal child and at puberty. Hercules was an aggressive, strong, partly divine man (son of Jupiter and the mortal Alcmene)—phallic, yet with bisexual tendencies. Gargantua was phallic and egregiously heterosexual; Gulliver, aside from his embarrassed and conflicted, exhibitionistic hyperawareness of the size of his genitals (both too big and too little to use) in relation both to the Lilliputians and the Brobdignagians, was asexual—with an especial aversion toward women as described in his reactions in Brobdignag and to the female Yahoos. But none of these giants could be ignored by the fathers of their or of this world.

Freud, through an association to the "open-air closet" dream, links it to the urination episode of the "Count Thun" dream. It was in connection with that part of the "Count Thun" dream (which comes earlier in the Dream book) that Freud first describes the

12. I have elsewhere (Shengold 1988) in a note on Freud and Rabelais pointed out the murderous hostility, masked by Rabelais' humor, involved in this urination, which drowned hundreds of Parisians. The linkage between murderous aggression and excretion, later to become a Freudian theme, is not alluded to in Freud's associations to this dream in 1900. Great ambition involves getting rid of, wanting to murder, those who stand in one's way.

incident of his urinating in the presence of his parents in their bedroom when he was seven. (In that dream Freud also brings in associations to Gargantua and Pantagruel—giant father and son). The father figure in that dream was an old man who

appeared to be blind, at all events with one eye, and I handed him a male glass urinal (which he had to buy or had bought in town). So I was a sick-nurse and had to give him the urinal because he was blind. . . . Here the man's attitude and his micturating penis appeared in plastic form. (This was the point at which I awoke, feeling a need to micturate). (1900, 210–11)

Freud connects this dream with his

megalomania of childhood. . . . It appears that when I was two years old I still occasionally wetted the bed, and when I was reproached for this I consoled my father by promising to buy him a nice new red bed in N., the nearest town of any size. (1900, 216)

And he brings in the scene at seven:

References to this scene are still constantly recurring in my dreams and are always linked [as in this dream] with an enumeration of my achievements and successes, as though I wanted to say: "You see, I *have* come to something." This scene, then, provided the material for the final episode of the dream, in which—in revenge, of course—the roles were interchanged. The older man (clearly my father, since his blindness in one eye referred to his unilateral glaucoma) was now micturating in front of me, just as I had in front of him in my childhood. In the reference to his glaucoma I was reminding him of the cocaine,[13] which had helped him in the operation, as though I had in that way kept my promise. Moreover, I was making fun of

13. Freud had narrowly missed fame as the discover of cocaine as an anaesthetic for eye operations. Freud had made suggestive comments on the plant's anaesthetic properties in his dissertation on coca, but, Freud said, he "had not been thorough enough to pursue the matter further" (1900b, 170). His friend Karl Koller had followed through on the suggestion after reading Freud's dissertation. Its use revolutionized eye surgery. Freud says, "Shortly after Koller's discovery, my father had in fact been attacked by glaucoma; my friend Dr. Königstein, the ophthalmic surgeon, had operated on him; while Dr. Koller had been in charge of the cocaine anaesthesia and had commented on the fact that this case had brought together all the three men who had had a share in the introduction of cocaine" (1900b, 171).

him; I had to hand him the urinal because he was blind, and [in my associations to the dream] I revelled in allusions to my discoveries in connection with the theory of hysteria, of which I felt so proud. (216–17)

Freud speaks of the "megalomanic train of thought" (471) that accompanies his associations to both dreams. He wrote this in 1900, when he had some feeling for his own greatness (he had the courage to compare himself to Copernicus and Darwin)[14] but had not yet achieved its recognition in the eyes of the world. The eyes are most important in Freud's rejoinder to the "world" of his childhood, father and mother: "You *see,* I have come to something" (1900, 217).

The mother (or at least someone's properly carrying out the functions of the mother) is usually more fundamental to the child's needs and sense of identity than the father, who, coming later in psychic development for the child, supplements her influence and can take over a preponderant part. In the "open-air closet" dream, both the "tiny queen" of Lilliput and the symbolic and allusive church of Notre Dame bring in the mother, co-witness to both the tiny boy's humiliation and the role-reversing fulfilled wishes of gigantic phallic and creative powers. Both parents, in their benevolent roles as nurturers and promoters of separation and achievement and as aspects of the child's ego ideals, contribute greatly to the child's achievement—alongside standing in his path.

Finally, confluent with his courage and his stoic drive toward the truth, is Freud's ability to see human existence as predominantly and ultimately tragic. This pessimistic tendency (one cannot of course separate this strength or indeed any of his gifts from Freud's neurotic complexes) does not dim his appreciation for the transient joys and glories of life. It does remind him of what we have to pay for our pleasures (he quotes the Rat Man's comments on experiencing sexual intercourse for the first time: "This is glorious! One might murder one's father for this!" [Freud 1909a, 210]). The challenge to indifference and evil coming both from the world outside ("the exigencies of reality" [Freud 1930, 139]) and from the world within the mind gives both Freud and his balanced, tragic view of life a heroic quality. He was able to recognize the psychic prevalence of incest, destructiveness, murder, cannibalism, and the

14. But not, even twenty years later, to Goethe.

unconscious guilt and search for punishment that results from the need to turn these instinctual forces against the self. Whatever the limitations of Freud's theory of the death instinct, he had the courage and clearsightedness to posit it. The wise and sad perspective of Freud's view of life (epitomized in *Civilization and Its Discontents* [1930] with its chastening view of the inevitability of compromise, of settling for less) can lead the frustrated, the frivolous, and the fearful to reject him as an ego ideal. Those who accept Freud's views need neither duplicate nor imitate them—but, if he is to be the ego ideal, one's own conception of the human condition ought to mirror the complexity of his.

I have in this book provided a sketch of Freud's life that is full of important gaps—for example, Freud's marriage, his relation to his children. I have dwelt on the unforgettable reproach from Freud's father when the boy was seven (1863), on the boy's ascendancy over his siblings in the eyes of his parents, on the relationships with Fliess (1887–1902), Jung (1907–13), Abraham (1907–26), on Freud's fantasy relation to Goethe and the biblical Joseph (who haunts *The Interpretation of Dreams* [1900]) and Moses (whom he wrote papers about in 1914 and 1933–39). I have not dealt with Freud's relationship with a very important father and older brother figure, Breuer, whom he acknowledged (unconvincingly) as a cofounder of psychoanalysis and who helped Freud financially and was so ambivalent about his ideas. To do justice to this complicated relationship would require access to the complete correspondence between the two men. I have neglected Freud's relationships with two son-figures, who defected from him in ways that he found personally very painful: Ferenczi and Rank. I would like to know much more than seems available about Freud's relations to his actual sons—why none of them followed their father's path to science or psychoanalysis. (It might have been harder for a son than for a daughter to compete with such a strong father—a father who seems to have felt more threatened by the competition of other males—but this is speculation.)

I have not adequately presented Freud's use of women as objects of his affections and drives, role models, and ego ideals. Women are less obvious in these capacities on the surface but not in the depths of his mind. Freud's mother was undoubtedly more important to him than was the father, about whom he wrote more. I assume that the discoverer of the Oedipus complex did not dwell on the inner picture, the psychic representation, of his mother as thoroughly in his introspection and his self-analysis as he did on that of his father. Freud's sisters do not seem ever to have great depth of meaning for him, although he was for the most part affectionate with, and dutiful toward, them. (In the family he came first in his parents' eyes and in his own.) Freud's mother died at ninety-five when he was in his mid-seventies. By that time he was of course in reality her caretaker rather than her dependent. As an old man he had in part outlived the emotional intensities inherent to conflicts both about his sexual and aggressive drives and his needs to be cared for. The feelings of dependency of course returned with the aging Freud's failings, infirmities, illnesses, and intimations of approaching death. He fought this regressive pull valiantly. As a young man, during his engagement, Freud both idealized and condescended to his fiancée, Martha. As a wife, she seems for a while to have taken over the central emotional role of the mother. But one gathers from his conversations and letters that there developed in Freud considerable dissatisfaction with at least some aspects of their relationship, and he wrote of himself in his forties as having given up his sexual life. (This of course could well have been an exaggeration but it was stated or intimated more than once.) In Freud's middle years there was a series of younger sister and especially daughter figures—Antigones—on whom he leaned for intellectual and emotional support, while Martha continued to administer wifely maternal care with great effectiveness. The series probably began with his sister-in-law, Minna, and it continued with pupils and patient-pupils like Ruth Mack Brunswick, Marie Bonaparte, Lou Andreas-Salomé, Helene Deutsch, and others. The most important female role in his inner life of fantasy during Freud's middle and last years was played by his daughter Anna. I am merely sketching Freud's relations with the women in his life and with the feminine. A full study of this (many have tried) would lack adequate documentation, especially from Freud's writings, in which fathers and brothers are featured. But the importance of women to Freud's identity, ideals, and theoretical ideas is beyond doubt. As we tend more and more to assume, from projections of early child development, from anthropological data, and from clinical psychoanalytic work, the mother goddesses were there before the sometimes more conspicuous father gods.

I find, in reviewing this last chapter, that I have repeatedly quoted two of my own teachers and ego ideals: Max Schur and

Lionel Trilling. I have quoted Trilling so often because I feel his pronouncements about Freud's moral qualities and influences are the most beautifully written and the most trenchant of any commentator's or biographer's—but I realize that I am still (to return to my first chapter) taking notes from my teacher.

In Chapter 7, I quoted Goethe's, "You see once again what is done for a man by a great predecessor, and the advantage of making a proper use of him" (Eckermann 1836, 173). The psychoanalyst and the psychotherapist of today have Freud as the "great predecessor" and need to make "proper use of him." Freud is "our" ego ideal. In the course of a psychoanalysis (or even of a psychotherapy) that works, the analyst can become a proper ego ideal: not the only, omniscient other, not the mirror image or Doppelgänger, not the primal parent, not the parent/breast who is a part of the self, not mother, not father, not an externalized conscience, not someone evoking overwhelming sexual excitement or murderous hatred. Although all of these roles can be transiently assigned in regression, the patient optimally takes leave of the analyst and has been able to, or soon becomes able to internalize—not the person of the analyst so much as the analytic attitude: the struggle to tolerate compromise, constraint, contradiction, complexity. The analyst as ego ideal can, for the most part, operate within the former patient's mind—as neither too much a part of the self nor too highly charged with instinctual wishes to compromise the autonomy (the separate will, judgment, and ability to integrate) of the patient.

Toward the end of his life, Freud urged all analysts to continue their efforts at self-analysis and even to go back periodically for reanalysis. This may not be necessary for all analysts; it is certainly not necessary for all analysands who have finished their analysis— and yet it is an important ideal. It exemplifies the way both Montaigne and Freud saw their lives and their life's work: as a continuing quest for self-knowledge, the idea of life as a continuing intellectual, emotional, and moral education.

CODA

VERSHININ: It seems to me there's no place on
earth, no matter how dull and depressing it may
be, where intelligent and educated people aren't
needed. Let's suppose that among the hundred
thousand people living here, there are just three
people like you—all the rest being uneducated and
uncultured. Obviously, you can't hope to win out
over the ignorance of the masses around you; in
the course of your life, you'll have to give in little
by little until you are lost in that crowd of one hundred thousand. Life will swallow you up, but not
completely, for you'll have made some impression.
After you've gone, perhaps there'll be six more people like you, then twelve, and so on, until finally
most people will have become like you. Why in two
or three hundred years life on this earth will be
wonderfully beautiful. Man longs for a life like
that, and if he doesn't have it right now, he must
imagine it, wait for it, dream about it, prepare for
it; he must know and see more than his father
and his grandfather did.

—Chekhov, *The Three Sisters*

I want to emphasize what is centrally related to Freud's tragic view
of life: murder—the NEED, as I see it, to kill off others.[1] The primal
situation of danger is the traumatic anxiety of overstimulation, that
affective too-muchness that threatens the very existence of self. I

1. Here is Freud's earliest word on murderous impulses. It is from a note
enclosed in a letter to Fliess dated May 31, 1897: "Impulses—Hostile impulses
against parents (a wish that they should die) are also an integral constituent of

see this fundamentally as an access of aggression, either as a reaction to the inexorable frustrations of reality for the immature infant
or, with Freud and (with special emphasis) Melanie Klein, as a
manifestation of a primary aggressive drive, or both. Overstimulation leads to murder. The danger and the drive require a caring,
caregiving other to mediate their vicissitudes: to fulfill needs, re-
store equilibrium, distance unbearable feelings. This other may
start as a part of the self ("I am the breast / the breast is part of
me");[2] but eventually it becomes a separated mothering person in
an initial global dichotomy; and ultimately mother, father, and
others are recognized, internalized, and registered within the mind
alongside the self as the most important part of mental structure
and contents. The first grandiose registrations (starting with
breast/me through omnipotent mother/me) evolve and can eventually be separated from a still narcissistic self.

This separation marks the beginning of object relations, which
in optimal development (in interplay with concomitant instinctual
and ego development) eventually reaches an oedipal period of
transformation and maturation. But since nothing in the mind is
ever lost, narcissistic object relations (the initial wish to be every-

neuroses. They come to light consciously as obsessional ideas. In paranoia what is
worst in delusions of persecution (pathological distrust of rulers and monarchs)
corresponds to these impulses. They are repressed at times when compassion for
the parents is active—at times of their illness or death. On such occasions it is a
manifestation of mourning to reproach oneself for their death (what is known as
melancholia) or to punish oneself in a hysterical fashion (through the medium of
the idea of retribution) with the same states [of illness] that they have had. . . . It
seems as though this death-wish is directed in sons against their fathers and daughters against their mothers" (1892–97, 254–55). Murderous impulses "as an integral
constituent of neuroses" is a preview of Freud's much later concept of aggression
as a drive. We are told in a footnote (by the editors of the *Origins of Psychoanalysis*
that Strachey copies in the Standard Edition of Freud) that the last sentence I have
quoted is "perhaps the very first hint at the Oedipus complex, which emerged in
full [in a letter to Fliess] some five months later" (255). Harold Blum remarked to
me that he feels Freud's statement about paranoia in this quotation is a foreshad-
owing of the currently prevalent idea of the central importance of preoedipal
(aggression-dominated or murderous) impulse in paranoia. A later statement: "The
primaeval history of mankind is filled with murder. Even today, the history of the
world which our children learn at school is essentially a series of murders of people"
(1915, 292).

2. Freud: "An infant at the breast does not as yet distinguish his ego from the
external world as the source of the sensations flowing in upon him. He gradually
learns to do so, in response to various promptings" (1930, 66–67).

thing and to be supplied with everything) will continue underneath and alongside[3] the subsequent burgeoning of mental structure and functioning that has such a crucial, rich, and dangerous course during the oedipal period. Everyone's oedipal period is a transformational phenomenon based on the particular preoedipal development that influences the transformation in varying individual ways. And everyone can and does regress defensively toward the narcissistic developmental positions which are retained at a variety of levels in individually varied intensity.

These regressions are evoked by major psychic danger situations, perhaps especially the primal one of traumatic overstimulation based, as I have said, on the presence of murderous aggressive feeling that cannot be tolerated. The basic clinical dilemma brought by every patient to life and to treatment is founded on the narcissistic paradox I have described (see Faimberg 1991). I would voice it this way: "I want to kill you, but I cannot live without you" (see Shengold 1991). This terrible contradiction is brought to the parent and parents and appears differently depending on the level of development that has been achieved. Murder is still there on the oedipal level (it is usually the part of the Oedipus complex that is hardest to deal with). One of my patients who had had incestuous contact with his mother used to say, "Fucking is murder"; he could have said, "Fucking is murdering mother." He would regress into anal narcissism, keeping a contemptuous emotional distance from others, in order basically to preserve the imago of his mother.

The impossible contradiction of needing to kill off the one you cannot survive without is made tolerable, as our murderous wishes regularly turned toward the self to protect others are made tolerable, by the capacity to love, to care for others and for the self; a capacity based on the very dependency we try to retreat from to maintain our narcissism. This capacity is derived from and involves dependency on and identification with a ministering mother figure, optimally an actual loving figure who can renounce her own needs

---

3. Freud: "In the realm of the mind . . . what is primitive is so commonly preserved alongside of the transformed version which has arisen from it that it is unnecessary to give instances as evidence. When this happens it is usually in consequence of a divergence in development: one portion (in the quantitative sense) of an attitude or instinctual impulse has remained unaltered, while another portion has undergone further development" (1930, 68–69).

sufficiently to encourage and take joy in the separate individuality of the child. Narcissism shrinks in tandem with incest and murder.

Lionel Trilling has written something that implies the universal continuing psychic influence of narcissism in our lives and how hard this is to resist. The essence of morality, he says, "is making a willing suspension of disbelief in the selfhood of someone else" (1955, 94). This suspension of disbelief is the vital step toward creating the other which can lead to loving another. Since our therapy and "cures" occur largely out of support and, perhaps, insight made possible by the acquisition of the power to care about another human being (why not call it love? [see Lear 1990]—the emotional force that can neutralize murder), this need to reduce narcissism is crucial for psychoanalysts.

All our lives, between the omnipotent claims and self-absorption of infancy and of old age, we need other people to continue the functions first performed by our primal parents and their internalized representations. Our psychic health and maturity depend in large part on what is called in psychoanalytic jargon the capacity for object relations—on our ability to get away from the original grandiose others who are part of ourselves so as to register other people as separate individuals whom we can care for and love.

Loving others is a transformation of the original union of child and ministering mother's breast:

> There is only one ["normal"] state—admittedly an unusual state, but not one that can be stigmatized as pathological—in which [. . . the ego does not maintain clear and sharp lines of demarcation]. At the height of being in love the boundary between ego and object threatens to melt away. Against all the evidence of his senses, a man who is in love declares the "I" and "you" are one, and is prepared to behave as if it were a fact. (Freud 1930, 66)

Freud is here talking of being in love as an unusual experience, and the passionate intensity of involvement in such a state (after all, dependent and therefore partially regressive) is different from the adult's more readily maintainable, experienced feeling of loving, in the sense of caring deeply about, others (which optimally but not necessarily accompanies being in love). I was recently at a lecture by the Israeli author Amos Oz who was asked by someone in the audience why there weren't more happy endings and more